INTELLIGENCE CAN BE TAUGHT

INTELLIGENCE CAN BE TAUGHT

Arthur Whimbey
with Linda Shaw Whimbey

A Sunrise Book

E. P. DUTTON & CO., INC. · NEW YORK · 1975

Grateful acknowledgment is made for permission to reprint the following copyright material: / From Carl Bereiter and Siegfried Engelmann, *Teaching Disadvantaged Children in the Preschool,* copyright © 1966 by Carl Bereiter and Siegfried Engelmann. Reprinted by permission of Prentice-Hall, Inc., Englewood Cliffs, N.J. / From Benjamin Bloom and Lois Broder, *Problem-Solving Processes of College Students,* copyright 1950 by Benjamin Bloom and Lois Broder. Reprinted by permission of the University of Chicago Press. / From *College Board Student Bulletin 1972–73,* p. 5. Reprinted by permission of College Entrance Examination Board, New York. / From *Effects of Coaching on Scholastic Aptitude Test Scores* (1965), pp. 14, 15. Reprinted by permission of College Entrance Examination Board, New York. / From Kurt Goldstein, *Human Nature in the Light of Psychopathology,* copyright 1940 by Kurt Goldstein. Reprinted by permission of Harvard University Press. / From Gary R. Gruber, *Reading Interpretation in Social Studies, Natural Sciences and Literature,* copyright © 1971 by Gary R. Gruber. Reprinted by permission of Simon and Schuster. / From Arthur Jensen, "Social Class and Verbal Learning," in *Social Class, Race, and Psychological Development,* edited by M. Deutsch, I. Katz, and A. R. Jensen, copyright © 1968 by M. Deutsch, I. Katz, and A. R. Jensen. Reprinted by permission of Holt, Rinehart and Winston. / From H. H. Newman, F. N. Freeman, and K. J. Holzinger, *Twins: A Study of Heredity and Environment,* copyright 1937 by H. H. Newman, F. N. Freeman, and K. J. Holzinger. Reprinted by permission of the University of Chicago Press. / From Thomas Pettigrew, *A Profile of the Negro American,* copyright © 1964 by Thomas Pettigrew. Reprinted by permission of D. Van Nostrand Co. / From Robert Rosenthal, "The Pygmalion Effect Lives," from *Psychology Today,* September, 1973, copyright © 1973 by Ziff-Davis Publishing Company. / From Miles A. Tinker, *Bases for Effective Reading,* copyright © 1965 by the University of Minnesota. Reprinted by permission of the University of Minnesota Press.

Library of Congress Cataloging in Publication Data

Whimbey, Arthur.
Intelligence can be taught.

"A Sunrise book."
Bibliography: p.
Includes index.
1. Intellect. 2. Mental tests. I. Whimbey, Linda Shaw, joint author. II. Title.
BF431.W53 1975 153.9'3 74-26931

 First Edition / 10 9 8 7 6 5 4 3 2 1 / *Published simultaneously in Canada by Clarke, Irwin & Company Limited, / Toronto and Vancouver / ISBN: 0-87690-128-3 / Dutton-Sunrise, Inc., a subsidiary of E. P. Dutton & Co., Inc. / Designed by The Etheredges*

For Clara Whimbey

ACKNOWLEDGMENT

This research was supported in part by a Special Postdoctoral Fellowship, # 1 F03 MH49391–01, from the National Institute of Mental Health, taken at the Institute of Human Learning, University of California, Berkeley.

I am also indebted to my editor, Marian Skedgell, for her patience, suggestions and encouragement in developing the manuscript.

CONTENTS

INTELLIGENCE CAN BE TAUGHT

I. CHANGES IN THE CONCEPT OF IQ

What do IQ tests really measure?

How can reasoning ability and reading comprehension skill be improved?

Does a person's intelligence develop from the experiences he has had since childhood—or is his intelligence primarily determined by the genes passed on to him from his parents?

These questions have been hotly debated since the first mental test was constructed at the turn of the century, but satisfactory answers have proved stubbornly elusive. Nevertheless, psychologists and educators have over the years accumulated an appreciable body of research on these questions, and within just the past decade a breakthrough seems to have occurred. Several experiments now appear to have isolated the mental activities that actually constitute intelligence. Other experiments have developed techniques for improving intelligence through training.

For example, in studies conducted at various major universities, the Stanford-Binet IQ test scores of culturally disadvantaged preschoolers have been substantially increased through programs of intensive tutoring. In one project, by means of daily training beginning in infancy, a group of children whose mothers had IQs under 75 achieved a mean IQ of 124. Another study, dealing with high school graduates, reported that following some 6 months of training, an overall average increase of 136 points was achieved on the nationally administered Scholastic Aptitude Test (SAT)—a test of adult mental ability, which has generally been regarded as resistant to direct training. In fact, further research indicated that for the majority of the young men involved in the study overall academic ability and college grades apparently also improved.

The various studies described in Chapter III present a convincing argument for the potential for mental growth through training. Nevertheless, it would be premature to conclude that the problem of training intelligence has been completely solved. Much additional research is needed.

What makes the experiments that have already been conducted so interesting is that, on the whole, they appear to be based on essentially the same concepts of intelligence and on closely related training procedures. Independently, different researchers have developed remarkably similar methods to increase the IQs of both preschoolers and young adults. Moreover, these experiments fit well with all our current information on what exactly intelligence is.

Psychologists regard psychometric instruments like the Stanford-Binet scale, the Wechsler test, the Army Alpha test, the SAT, and the Graduate Record Exam (GRE) basically as tests of intelligence. Some psychologists more guardedly label them *academic aptitude* examinations because they are frequently used in predicting academic performance and because researchers have been unable to pinpoint and explain precisely what it is they do measure. Common agreement exists, however, on two points: first, that these tests gauge some mental attribute that is critical to academic success and that is important in many vocations, especially the professions; and second, that this measurable human attribute, commonly called intelligence, appears to be only minimally bettered by current educational practices.

For several years now, Arthur Jensen, of the University of California, has used the second point to bolster his argument that intelligence is almost entirely inherited and fixed by genetic chemistry. Christopher Jencks, of Harvard, who has compiled the most comprehensive statistical study ever made of the heritability question, has come to a sharply different conclusion. His data, presented in his book *Inequality,* indicate that mental capacity depends in large part on experiential and environmental factors, but that educators have not yet been able to establish a direct correlation between any of these factors and the development of intelligence. That this should be so is not really surprising. Mass education is, after all, a fairly recent human invention, and educators have only recently begun to explore alternate formats and methods.

DEVELOPMENT OF THE STANFORD-BINET IQ TEST

Modern intelligence testing had its start in 1904, when the Parisian minister of education asked Alfred Binet to construct a test that would identify slow learners so that they could be placed in special remedial classes. Binet, who joined the psychological laboratory at the Sorbonne in 1892 and became its director in 1894, had for years researched alternative procedures for gauging mental capacity. Measures of sensory discrimination (such as the ability to judge line length accurately), reaction time, even cranial size were explored and discarded. Finally, a selection of items was compiled that directly measured comprehension, judgment, and reasoning. In 1905, Binet and his coworker, Théodore Simon, produced the first successful intelligence test, designed for use with children aged 3 to 11 years. The scale was revised in 1908, and its range was increased to age 13. Another revision was completed in 1911 (the year of Binet's death), with a few test items reaching to the adult level. At about this time, Lewis Terman, of Stanford University, translated and adapted Binet's scale for American use and extended it so it could be effectively employed with adults. Terman's work culminated in the Stanford-Binet test of 1916, followed by new editions in 1937 and 1960.

The Stanford-Binet is still today the recognized standard of IQ measurement. While many other tests have followed in its path, it remains the one most widely used in research studies, and it occupies a central position in the heredity-environment controversy. Its composition varies somewhat with age level. Primarily it measures verbal comprehension and verbal reasoning, plus a smattering of mathematical reasoning, spatial reasoning, and figural reasoning. The following test items are similar to those of the Stanford-Binet:

4-YEAR-OLD LEVEL

PICTURE VOCABULARY: Child names pictured objects, such as a fork.

NAMING OBJECTS FROM MEMORY: A toy automobile, a spoon, and a toy cat are placed in front of the child, and he is helped to name them. One is then removed while the child's eyes are closed, and when he reopens his eyes he is asked to name the missing object.

OPPOSITE ANALOGIES: Father is a man, mother is a ______.

COMPREHENSION: Child is asked, "Why do we have cars?"

DISCRIMINATION OF FORM: Child matches or classifies circles, squares, and triangles.

6-YEAR-OLD LEVEL

VOCABULARY: What is an apple?

DIFFERENCES: What is the difference between a cat and a horse?

MAZE TRACING: Child traces the shortest route through a maze.

NUMBER CONCEPTS: Child gives the examiner 10 blocks.

MUTILATED PICTURES: What part of this picture is missing?

OPPOSITE ANALOGIES: An elephant is heavy, a mouse is ______.

ADULT AND SUPERIOR ADULT LEVELS

VOCABULARY: Examinee is asked to define selected words such as *misanthrope* and *parquet.*

ESSENTIAL DIFFERENCES: Explain the difference between *potential* and *accomplishment.*

ARITHMETICAL REASONING: Three envelopes cost 5 cents. How many can be purchased for 35 cents?

PROVERB INTERPRETATION: What does "a stitch in time saves nine" mean?

ORIENTATION: If you are facing east and then turn left, which direction is behind you?

MINKUS COMPLETION (SENTENCE COMPLETION): Fill in the blanks. He is taller______his brother, but he weighs______.

INGENUITY: A man has a 2-qt. can and a 7-qt. can. How can he measure out exactly 1 qt. of water?

REPEATING THOUGHT OF PASSAGE: A short paragraph is read to the examinee, and he is required to recall it as best he can. Scoring is based on the recall of ideas, not exact wording.

As the above examples indicate, in the Stanford-Binet, nonverbal problems (such as Maze Tracing and Mutilated Pictures) are confined mainly to the younger age levels. Lewis Terman, who developed the Stanford-Binet, believed that comprehension and reasoning with verbal concepts were the highest expressions of intelligence, and so at the adult levels the Stanford-Binet is almost completely verbal in content. Other intelligence tests, such as the Wechsler and the Lorge-Thorndike, include more nonverbal problems at the adult level, and the Raven Matrices test consists entirely of nonverbal problems.

The Stanford-Binet is an individual intelligence test: An

examiner tests only one person at a time. This is frequently necessary in clinical work and with young children. World War I, however, created a need for an IQ measure that could be administered to a large group of persons simultaneously. A committee headed by Robert Yerkes quickly produced the Army Alpha test, modeled on the Stanford-Binet. Many Binet-type items were rewritten in multiple-choice format for group testing, and other types of items were added.

Following the war, the Army Alpha was adapted for civilian use by schools and employers, and group testing of intelligence became a regular and widespread practice.

THE SO-CALLED ACADEMIC APTITUDE TESTS

The SAT—familiar to most college students—is a direct descendant of the Stanford-Binet and the Army Alpha tests. It is a group mental test used to help admissions officers select those high school graduates who will be admitted to certain colleges. Thus its purpose parallels the original Binet test, which was used for classification of elementary school pupils.

The content of the SAT is almost identical to that of the adult-level Stanford-Binet. It is divided into a Verbal Section and a Quantitative Section. The Verbal Section contains four subtests: Vocabulary, Verbal Analogies, Sentence Completion, and Reading Comprehension. Examples of the first three of these items appear above. The fourth subtest, Reading Comprehension, is related to the Stanford-Binet item called Repeating Thought of Passage.

The Quantitative Section of the SAT is composed primarily of arithmetical reasoning and algebra word problems. It resembles what is called Ingenuity and Arithmetical Reasoning in the Stanford-Binet, but requires some knowledge of algebra.

There is a common misconception that the Stanford-Binet measures innate mental capacity, whereas academic aptitude tests such as the SAT are more heavily dependent on learning.

This is obviously impossible, since the items in the adult Stanford-Binet and the items in the SAT (especially in the Verbal Section) are almost identical. In fact, statistical studies show that scores on the Stanford-Binet correlate as highly with the SAT as they do with any other traditional IQ test (such as the Wechsler), indicating that all such tests measure basically the same mental abilities. Thus, for example, in her book *Psychological Testing,* Anne Anastasi discusses the SAT in the chapter entitled "Group Tests of General Intelligence."

The only real difference between the Stanford-Binet and the SAT is that the Stanford-Binet score is reported as an IQ, whereas each section of the SAT is reported as a scaled score that ranges from 200 to 800, with a mean of about 500.

The Graduate Record Exam (GRE) and the Law School Admission Test (LSAT), discussed in subsequent chapters, are basically upward extensions of the SAT. They measure primarily the same abilities, but at a higher level of difficulty. The GRE is used to select from among college seniors those who will be admitted to graduate school, and the LSAT is used for law school admission decisions. The differences between the tests are small in comparison with their similarities. The SAT, GRE, and LSAT are all constructed by the Educational Testing Service, although an affiliated company, the College Entrance Examination Board, governs administrative policies concerning the SAT.

OBSOLESCENCE OF THE TERM IQ

Mental testing began when Binet developed a scale to classify young children into educational groupings. From this start, the idea of *mental age* readily developed. It was based on the following rationale:

Suppose that the test score of a certain 12-year-old was not as high as the *average* score of a typical group of 12-year-olds. Suppose, instead, that his score was equal to the average of a group of 9-year-olds. This youngster was regarded as having the mentality of a 9-year-old, and he was said to have a mental age of 9. The next step was to take the ratio of his mental age to his chronological age and obtain his intelligence quotient, or IQ. Thus:

$$IQ = \frac{\text{mental age}}{\text{chronological age}} \times 100^{*} = \frac{9}{12} \times 100 = 75$$

As another example, a child who was only 6 years old, but had a mental age of 9 on the test, had an IQ of 150.

$$IQ = \frac{9}{6} \times 100 = 150$$

A third child, whose test score was exactly equal to the average of his age group, had an IQ of 100.

The IQ notion, which Binet vigorously opposed, was based on the assumption that mental capacity is a simple unitary dimension such as height. Thus it was believed that children of different ages could be directly compared with one another and even that adults could be directly compared with children along the same mental scale. This assumption has proved false.

It is now recognized that a 12-year-old with a mental age of 9 generally has a different pattern of mental skills and abilities from those of a 6-year-old with a mental age of 9. Carl Bereiter emphasized this in devising his preschool program for poverty children. He observed that the low IQ scores of culturally disadvantaged children result primarily from those test items that depend on their having already learned concepts and skills relevant to educational progress. On these items they score below the national average for their age levels. But on items that measure raw learning and memory capacity, such children perform fully up to standard. Thus,

*The quotient of mental age to chronological age is multiplied by 100 to eliminate the decimal point.

their overall IQ scores present a distorted picture of their educational potential.

Similarly, it is never appropriate to regard an adult with a low IQ as having the mental ability of a child. Depending on his background, an adult may score low on certain tests of IQ; but in other respects his mental ability will invariably be different from that of a child.

The human nervous system does not reach full maturity until approximately 13 years after birth, and until then physiological limitations restrict thinking capacity. This is clearly illustrated in Jean Piaget's research. For example, Piaget observed that before the age of 8 a child may believe a *tall* narrow 1-qt. cylinder holds more liquid than a *short* thick one, even after he has seen a quart of liquid transferred from one cylinder to the other and back again. The child is not able to separate the idea of quantity from the immediate perception of height—he is not yet capable of what Piaget calls "conservation of quantity." Furthermore, total "conservation of volume" does not develop until age 12. By contrast, normal adults, irrespective of their IQs, have no trouble with such primary discriminations. J. McVicker Hunt elaborated on this point in *Intelligence and Experience.* He noted that since all adults (except the feebleminded) appear capable of Piaget's formal operations, individual differences in adult intelligence are apparently not comparable to the differences that occur in children as a consequence of growth. Instead, variations in adult intelligence reflect different aptitudes in the use of formal operations. These differences arise from contrasting opportunities for learning.

Differences among adults in intelligence are based on a pattern of learned information-processing skills. These skills may begin to develop in early childhood if encouraged by the appropriate home or school environment, but they can also be taught directly to adults.

A child's mental ability (or academic aptitude) is dependent both on his mastery of these information-processing skills and on the stage of his neural development. Whereas all healthy adults seem to be approximately equal in neural potential, children grow to this adult level at different rates. They may even show distinct spurts of growth at different ages. Such differences must be reckoned with in comparing the abilities of children and in designing educational programs.

The complex nature of mental ability has made the use of the overall IQ score totally obsolete. Because of this, neither the Wechsler test nor the new Stanford-Binet test employs the traditional IQ: In neither case is an individual's score compared with the average score of different age groups. Furthermore, the ratio of mental age to chronological age is never computed in obtaining the IQ. However, the term IQ is deeply entrenched in psychology and education—teachers and test administrators are accustomed to using it. And so the constructors of the Wechsler and Stanford-Binet tests were compelled to provide some sort of IQ number rather than just a standardized test score. Accordingly, they invented a purely statistical *deviation IQ.* This changeover is explained further in all textbooks on mental measurement.

The term IQ will, no doubt, gradually fade from use. It is, however, frequently used today and so it is retained here to facilitate communication. It is not employed in its original sense of directly comparing the mental abilities of adults and children, or of children of different ages, but only as a synonym for *intelligence, academic aptitude,* or—perhaps best of all —*scholastic readiness* in referring to that mental ability which is common to the various widely used intelligence tests.

HEALTHY INTELLIGENCE DISTINCT FROM NEURAL PATHOLOGY

Psychometrists now recognize that an important distinction must be made between the type of mental incapacity that results from neurological injury or disease and the type characteristic of organically healthy persons of low IQ. Failure to recognize and understand this distinction has hindered progress in devising IQ-training programs for organically healthy children and adults.

A healthy person of low IQ shows certain deficiencies in advanced problem solving, but these deficiencies differ in kind from those found among persons with true neurological pathology. One example, drawn from Kurt Goldstein's writings, is cited here to illustrate the difference; additional examples are discussed in Chapter VI.

Goldstein has presented a vivid picture of the inability of patients with brain lesions to think abstractly. First, he described what he meant by abstract thinking:

> Our behavior is abstract when we give a name to an object. When we speak of "table" we do not mean a special given table with all its accidental properties; we mean table in general. The word is used as a representative of the category "table."

Brain lesions of a certain type disrupt a person's ability to think in this way:

> Asked to mention the names of several different kinds of animals, the patient may be at first unable to do so. In one case it was not until we had given a patient such examples as dog, cat, mouse, that she replied to the question at all. Then suddenly she said: "A polar bear; a brown bear; a lion; a tiger." Asked why she named these particular animals, she said, "If we enter the zoological gardens, we come at first to the polar bear and then to the other animals." Obviously she had recalled the animals as they were situated in the zoological gardens, and had used the words only as belonging to the concrete situation, not as names for objects. It was very characteristic that she did not simply say "bear," a word which represents the category of all bears, and which we would use when asked to name animals, but that instead she selected the words "polar bear," "brown bear."

Goldstein continued in a later section:

> How very concretely such words are apprehended may be demonstrated by the following example. When, to such a patient of ours, a knife was offered with a pencil, she called the knife a "pencil sharpener"; when the knife was offered with an apple, it was to her an "apple parer"; when offered with a potato, it was a "potato peeler"; in company with a piece of bread, it became a "bread knife"; and with a fork it was "knife and fork." The word "knife" alone she never uttered spontaneously, and when she was asked, "Could we not always call it simply knife?" she replied promptly, "No."

The syndrome described by Goldstein arises from a brain lesion and seriously impairs thinking capacity and intelligence. However, it is unique to this type of neural pathology and is not a factor in healthy persons, even when their IQ scores are low. All healthy adults are capable of the basic abstractions Goldstein discussed. By the same token, other forms of neurologically based retardation—whether congenital, as in the case of mongolism, or arising from postnatal injury or disease—involve different mechanisms and, in general, more severe limitations than the type of low academic intelligence on which this book focuses. Fortunately, the majority of low IQ scores are of the latter type. They are not founded in neurological defect and are highly receptive to training.

II. THE BLIND SIDE OF PSYCHOMETRICS

Because so few experimental studies have shown that intelligence can be improved through training, many conclude that intelligence is untrainable. Such a conclusion is unwarranted. There is no long list of experimental projects that have attempted and then failed to increase IQ. The simple truth is that very few projects have actually tried to train IQ.

One deterrent to research has been the pervasive assumption that genetic influences exert a strong and unmodifiable effect in dictating mental capacity. In Chapter VI the pertinent studies on the genetics of human intelligence are examined. They supply little basis for this assumption.

Certain traditions and orientations in American psychology also have hindered the development of cognitive training methods. For example, in his 1957 presidential address to the American Psychological Association, Lee J. Cronbach noted that the two subareas of psychology that are most closely related to the problems of human intellect—the subareas called *psychometrics* and *experimental learning*—have tended to maintain separate paths and interests.

Psychometrics, as the name suggests, is the branch of psychology concerned with psychological measurement—primarily the measurement of thinking abilities and aptitudes. Accordingly, psychometrists have concentrated their efforts on test construction, statistical refinement, and test administration. These are important enterprises, which have contributed materially to modern technological growth. But there has been a relative neglect, on the part of psychometrists, of systematic research into the development and the training of the mental capacities that are now measurable with fair accuracy. The psychometrist's domain has been narrowly defined as the scaling of crystallized abilities. Insights about human abilities that might be gained from extended training studies have been closed off to psychometrists. As a result, testers and guidance counselors have been left without remedial methods to help improve an individual's cognitive weaknesses after they have been identified through testing.

Experimental learning psychologists, on the other hand, have conducted studies investigating the conditions of human learning. But they have frequently shunned complex reasoning of the type most relevant to academic achievement. Instead, there has been an overabundance of studies of simple learning—the learning and recall of lists of words, nonsense syllables, and digits. Of course, some studies on complex learning and cognition have been undertaken (concept formation, learning sets, learning to learn, perception and processing of information), but such studies have been all too few.

In their presidential addresses to the American Psychological Association, Cronbach in 1957 and Donald Hebb in 1960 called for a rapprochement, a communication and unity of purpose, between experimentalists and psychometrists in order that quicker progress might be brought to educational theory. But such changes occur only gradually. Eight years later, in the preface to *Social Class, Race and Psychological Development* (published in 1968), Ernest Hilgard, a prominent learning theorist, made the following observations:

> In recent years there has been such a celebration of "basic research" that the criterion of relevance to important problems has receded, and many behavioral and social scientists find satisfaction in building elaborate theoretical models around

> precise but somewhat irrelevant data. Hence when colleagues who attempt to face up to social problems look for relevant data and hypotheses, they often do not find much that they can use. Not unrelated to the emphasis upon basic science is the tendency to specialize. Even within psychology, the subspecialties of behavior genetics, physiology of learning, social psychology, clinical psychology, and educational psychology become encapsulated and thus less accessible to the kind of team effort that is essential to the solving of social problems.

Psychology is a young science, having yet to celebrate its centennial. Compare it, for example, with the study of human biology and medicine. William Harvey elucidated the circulation of the blood and the function of the heart more than 350 years ago, and his contribution was preceded by centuries of organized medical practice. Nevertheless, the full understanding and cure of heart disease are still but a hope for the future —a hope, we might note, that is supported by huge and well-endowed research foundations.

In fact, enormous progress has been made by psychologists in defining the mechanisms of human and animal behavior. However, it is crucial to recognize that the absence of fully developed procedures for training intelligence stems from the immaturity of the sciences of psychology and pedagogy—not from the proved impossibility of the task. The conclusion of some educators (such as Arthur Jensen) that "compensatory education has been tried and it apparently has failed" is not only premature, but completely untrue. The surface has only been scratched. The possibilities have hardly been conceived, much less tried.

BEHAVIORISM IN PSYCHOMETRICS

Historically, there has been one other evident block to intelligence-training research—the tendency (until recently) for American psychology to emphasize *behaviorism* and to exclude introspection as a method for collecting psychological data.

Fostered around 1920 by John B. Watson, behaviorism is the doctrine that a psychologist must concern himself *only* with external behavior; under no circumstances may he introspect regarding his own thought processes and mental activities, nor may he request or use the introspective reports of others. A person's thoughts can be directly observed by no one but himself—they are not open to public view by the scientific community—and thus they cannot serve as legitimate data for a "true" science of psychology. So says behaviorism.

Banning introspection is not an established and basic principle of science; no other science has had to face exactly this issue. Yet this proscription has effectively outlawed research projects that might systematically question capable problem solvers regarding their mental activities and then attempt to teach these same mental activities to those who show ineptitude in the area. Herbert Simon, one of the originators of computer chess-playing programs (he also designed a program called "Logic Theorist" for proving theorems in symbolic logic), observed that luckily his professional background had not been in the traditional American psychology of the 1940s and 1950s—or he might not have felt free to interview chess masters about their game strategies in gathering information for the computer. In fact, "thinking-aloud" procedures furnished a major part of the data for Allen Newell and Herbert Simon's insightful book, *Human Problem Solving.*

The dear price of behaviorism was described by the renowned educator, Benjamin Bloom, in a neglected little book (coauthored by Lois Broder), *The Problem-Solving Processes of College Students:*

> Mental processes represent a very difficult and complex subject for study. To a large extent, we have been limited in this study by the wide-spread emphasis on overt behavior as the major

acceptable type of evidence on the workings of the mind. Much of psychological research attempts to infer from the observed behavior of the individual what the mental processes must have been. This attempt to make an objective science of psychology not only limits the kinds of data acceptable to the psychologist but must necessarily make for many inaccuracies in his inferences about the nature of the mental processes.

The handicap placed on the work of the psychologist by the type of data he regards as useful and scientific is well demonstrated in the field of individual differences. Much of the work in this field is based on the use of various types of tests. In these tests the subject is presented with questions which he is to answer and problems which he is to solve. After some mental effort, the subject submits his answers or solutions for appraisal by the tester. In addition, the tester may secure observations of the behavior of the subject while taking the test. From these data the tester will attempt to draw conclusions about the mental characteristics of the subject. What is missing is information on the process by which the problems are solved. The methods of attack, the steps in the thinking processes, the kinds of considerations used to make one choice rather than another, and the feelings and attitudes of the subject are neglected or given very little attention. The products of thought —the answers to the questions or the solutions to the problems —plus the observations may give the tester a fleeting glimpse into the complex processes of thought involved, but usually this is incomplete and, almost of necessity, inaccurate.

Bloom and Broder went on to make the following observation:

It should be noted that concern about processes of thought is evident in the work of some educators and psychologists. In schools where tutorial methods and small-class discussion methods are utilized, the instructor is frequently as much concerned about the student's methods of thinking as about the results of the thinking.

We shall see in Chapter III that such methods are exactly those that have produced experimental increases in IQ test scores and academic aptitude.

It is noteworthy that the two greatest contributors to our knowledge of intelligence—Binet and Piaget—were Europeans who made extensive use of introspection.* In his 1894 experimental psychology book *(Introduction à la psychologie expérimentale),* Binet warned against an overdependence on statistical studies in cognition research. Instead, he suggested greater use of introspective reports from several subjects, collated to distill the common processes of human thinking. American psychometrists have unduly limited their theoretical perspective by leaning too heavily on correlational analyses, statistical analyses, and factor analyses of test scores, which are themselves the end products of thinking. In consequence, the psychometrists have left themselves vulnerable to such critics of IQ testing as Carl Senna (in *The Fallacy of I.Q.),* who claim that a major deficiency of psychometric science today is a glaring absence of subject matter. The alternative, needed to bring a balance to psychometric science, has been described by Bloom and Broder:

> An investigation of thought-processes would probably mean that the psychologist must study relatively small numbers of subjects under adequately controlled conditions rather than make the large-scale type of study ordinarily employed in investigations of individual differences.

*Strictly speaking (as noted by Bloom and Broder), much of Piaget's work involved examination of children's spontaneous talk during problem solving and a form of retrospection—having children answer questions about how and why they arrived at a certain answer to a problem. The comparative utility of introspection and these other procedures—as methods of investigating mental processes through verbal reports—may be a topic for future research.

PROGRAMS THAT FAILED TO IMPROVE INTELLIGENCE

Two educational research projects have at times been cited as proving that attempts to improve intelligence are bound to fail. One of these involved an evaluation of coaching for academic aptitude examinations.

The Educational Testing Service and the College Entrance Examination Board (which together administer the SAT, GRE, and LSAT) publish statements like the following:

> The College Board suggests that students not invest time and money on special drilling or coaching programs. Time spent on general reading and school assignments will prove at least as beneficial in preparing for the SAT and far more beneficial in preparing for college.

Since academic aptitude tests are seen by many as the gatekeepers to advanced education and financial reward—admission to college, graduate school, and law school depends on high scores—highly advertised cram courses, as well as many legitimate schools, offer short-term practice programs, which, the student is told, may serve to increase his test scores. In the interest of fairness to all students, the College Board (and other testing organizations in the United States and Britain) ran a series of careful evaluative experiments to determine just how effective such coaching programs really are.

The typical program began with a brief description of the types of items used on entrance exams. Students then attempted sample problems and were told whether or not their answers were correct. Sometimes a brief refresher course in arithmetic and algebra was offered. A pamphlet, *Effects of Coaching on Scholastic Aptitude Test Scores,* published by the College Board, described one such study as follows:

> At school A only the regular courses were pursued, and no attempt was made to coach the students for the SAT. Students

at this school provided the experimental control group for studies of both the SAT-verbal and SAT-mathematical score changes.

At school B, the 126 students involved in the study had the following coaching on verbal materials in the winter semester: an average of 90 minutes on the school's special 500-word vocabulary list; an average of 90 minutes with vocabulary and reading comprehension materials in a commercially published English review book; an average of 90 minutes with sample verbal questions like those used in the SAT. Of these students, there were 44 who were planning to take the SAT in connection with their applications for college admission. These 44 undertook additional study of about two hours with the English review book and about two hours with three commercial publications on how to prepare for college entrance tests. School B students received no extra instruction or coaching in mathematics.

At school C the 188 college preparatory and technical students participating in the study were coached throughout the winter semester with both verbal and mathematical materials. These materials consisted of 20 special exercises made up of items specially prepared at Educational Testing Service to resemble items on the SAT. The exercises were worked in class and discussed immediately. There were 39 students who expected to take the SAT for college admission, and these 39 were given extra drill on mathematics problems. Shortly before the March 1955 administration of the SAT all 188 students took a 40-minute practice test of verbal items and a 40-minute practice test of mathematical items.

In March 1955 the students in all three schools took the SAT again.

It was found that the average scores for various groups of the coached students had increased from September to March more than the average scores of the corresponding groups of uncoached students. The differences in score gains were comparatively small, however.

These differences are shown in Table 1.

TABLE 1.
DIFFERENCES IN AVERAGE SAT SCORE GAINS OF COACHED AND UNCOACHED STUDENTS

	AVERAGE SCORE GAIN DIFFERENCES	
Verbal	*School C minus School A*	*School B minus School A*
Boys	15.2 (.02)	−1.7
Girls	22.4 (.01)	12.3
Boys and girls	18.3 (.01)	5.0 (.05)
	AVERAGE SCORE GAIN DIFFERENCES	
Mathematical	*School C minus School A*	*School C minus School B*
Boys not taking mathematics	9.3	29.2 (.05)
Girls not taking mathematics	.9	4.2
Boys taking mathematics	5.0	18.8 (.05)
Girls taking mathematics	20.2	29.7 (.05)
All boys and girls	6.2 (.01)	18.0 (.01)

NOTES: *Students at School A were not coached. Students at School B were coached in verbal material only. Students at school C were coached in both verbal and mathematical material.*

Differences in average score gains are expressed in points on the College Board score scale of 200–800. Positive numbers show differences in favor of the coached groups. The two-place decimals in parentheses after some of the gains indicate the probability that those gains could have occurred by chance. The decimal .02, for example, may be read as "there are no more than 2 chances in 100 that the foregoing result could have occurred by chance." Differences not followed by such decimals could have occurred by chance more than 5 times out of 100 and are therefore not considered statistically significant.

SOURCE: *College Entrance Examination Board, 1965.*

Experiments of this sort have led to the conclusion that coaching has but a minor effect on scores, too small to appreciably influence admission decisions. But a difficulty arises when such studies are taken as evidence that intelligence is untrainable—which is exactly what a number of educators and writers, such as Arthur Jensen, have done. These studies must be seen for what they are. Their purpose was not to analyze academic aptitude in an attempt to develop effective instructional techniques; their goal was only to evaluate popularly used "practice" programs—a pragmatic and useful, but theoretically narrow, goal. The experiment described above illustrates this well.

At school B there were 90 minutes of coaching in one area, 90 minutes in another area, and 2 hours in a third. This was obviously and intentionally just a hodgepodge of commercial cram programs.

Training at school C was apparently more lengthy, although still quite limited. Furthermore, the exact training procedure was not reported. In Chapter III we shall see that factors such as training method, class size, and extent of training play an important role in determining how effective an intelligence-training program is. Yet, in spite of the inadequate consideration given to such factors, Table 1 shows that the school C program did increase SAT scores to a statistically significant degree. On the basis of this information we must conclude that while the effects of limited coaching are not large, they do indicate that continued research to devise better training methods would be worthwhile.

In none of the coaching programs studied was individual attention given to the manner in which a student's approach to problems was in error. Nor was any detailed instruction supplied in the mental behaviors (the specific focus, discriminations, and directions of thought) leading to a correct solution. For example, practice for reading comprehension tests did not include personal guidance in the interpretation of sentences and paragraphs so that the student could learn the fundamental processes of progressively reconstructing an author's meaning. Instead, there was only a broad and brief discussion of the errors the student made on comprehension questions. The procedure was analogous to a golf instructor's standing by the cup and informing the novice where his ball landed—"a little to the left" or "somewhat short and to the right"—instead of showing the proper hand positioning and grasp, demonstrating the exact stance of the feet and legs, and then taking the student in hand and letting him feel the correct movement and arc of the swing.

Thus, while the studies conducted by the College Entrance Examination Board, the Educational Testing Service, and other organizations served the useful purpose of evaluating existing coaching programs, they can hardly be considered primary research on training mental ability, since in fact they made no attempt to explore and develop new methods for teaching intelligence.

PROJECT HEAD START

Head Start, which attempted to increase intelligence through environmental manipulations, has also been viewed as a failure. Arthur Jensen (among others) has used this to argue against the expenditure of federal monies on compensatory education for children from low-income homes.

Head Start sought to raise the IQs of culturally deprived youngsters through "environmental enrichment." A sample of preschoolers from low-income families and ghetto areas was selected to attend "stimulating" nursery schools for 1 or 2 years before entering the first grade. As a result, they made gains of between 5 and 10 points on IQ tests. But the gains were short-lived and tended to disappear within the first year of regular schooling.

In retrospect, it is clear that Head Start was based on a painfully vague theoretical foundation. There were no relevant experimental data on the effectiveness of this type of program. It was a shot-in-the-dark approach that hoped to simulate the middle-class home environment. Had the approach worked, it would have been wonderful—it would also have been miraculous. In point of fact, the children had spent the earliest years of their lives completely under the home influence, they returned to the ghetto every evening and weekend, and after their 1 or 2 years in Head Start they were returned permanently to the ghetto with its poverty, pessimism, and skeptical disrespect for education. In trying to give them middle-class home advantages, without a scientifically based pedagogical rationale, Head Start was certain to be less than a complete success.

A sharp contrast to Head Start is seen in Israeli kibbutzim. Outside the kibbutz the children of Oriental Jews average 85 on IQ tests, children of European Jews average 105. Within the kibbutz both groups average 115. The kibbutz offers a much more complete equalization of cultural influences than that provided by Head Start.

Nevertheless, such complete environmental control may not be absolutely necessary in nurturing mental growth. Increases in IQ through limited but direct cognitive training have been achieved and documented, as will be shown in the next chapter.

III. COGNITIVE THERAPY: NEW APPROACHES TO TRAINING INTELLIGENCE

Recent studies that have specifically concerned themselves with analyzing and improving mental capacity have given highly promising results. All but one of the studies reviewed in this chapter have been conducted since McVicker Hunt's 1961 landmark book, *Intelligence and Experience.* The one exception (Bloom and Broder's) has been virtually lost to educational psychology since its publication in 1950.

The various experiments differ in some respects and are redundant in others. Some researchers have tried to identify the childhood experiences responsible for low academic intelligence, while other researchers have focused exclusively on remedial measures. Nevertheless, a common thread of rationale and methodology runs through all the experiments. The training procedures used, with both children and adults, are in many ways similar. The general approach I have labeled *cognitive therapy.*

Most of the preschool remedial programs described in the following pages were aimed specifically at children from low-income black families because the civil rights awareness of the 1960s and 1970s has insisted that racial prejudice and vocational inequality in America be eliminated. However, the training procedures that have emerged from these civil-rights-oriented research projects are as applicable to white children with depressed IQs as they are to black children with depressed IQs.

RUPERT KLAUS AND SUSAN GRAY, GEORGE PEABODY COLLEGE FOR TEACHERS

In 1962, Klaus and Gray began an attack on the problem confronting many youngsters from socioeconomically depressed homes. These children begin school at an intellectual disadvantage—and then undergo a further progressive decline in IQ and relative scholastic achievement as they move through the elementary grades.

Several aspects of the poverty culture appeared to combine in putting slum children at an academic disadvantage. For one thing, Klaus and Gray found an extensive degree of physical disorganization in many slum homes; there was a lack of spatial and temporal stability that appeared to be a handicap to cognitive development. But a more important effect of the life circumstances of poverty children related to language growth. The language of the children with whom Klaus and Gray worked was conspicuously retarded, and this appeared to stem from the types of verbal exchanges occurring in the home. Klaus and Gray presented the following description:

> The mother will talk little to the child, and, even more importantly, she will not listen to the child. When she talks, it is apt to be in a "restricted code," to use Bernstein's term (1961). A restricted code is one in which most of the meaning must be carried by other aspects of the total situation: facial expression, intonation rather than words spoken, the circumstances. The child, thus, does not learn to use language effectively. Contrast this situation with that in the middle-class home, where the mother listens to and reinforces the language of her child and, typically, will elaborate upon the child's early language. Thus, "Kitty scratch!" becomes "Yes, kitty will scratch you with her claws, if you pull her by her tail."

Klaus and Gray initiated an experimental program, named the Early Training Project, that attempted to ameliorate this situation. Three-year-old black children from Nashville and the adjacent area participated in the study. Nineteen children attended three 10-week summer sessions that met for 4 hours a day, 5 days a week, over three consecutive summers. A primary characteristic of the program was the use of several instructors and the formation of subgroups (with a low 5:1 student-teacher ratio). This arrangement allowed a great deal of verbal interaction and permitted the teacher to pay attention to each child's development in perceptual discrimination ability, concept formation, number ability, and language.

Standard nursery school materials were available—wheeled toys, blocks, puzzles, easel paints—but they were used to encourage the development of cognitive skills. For example, the child was taught to request use of a tricycle with increasingly greater exactitude and complexity. At first the child simply learned to formulate a complete sentence. Later he was required to specify which tricycle—the little green one. And if the tricycle was being used by another child, he learned to ask the other child if he might take a turn. As another example, 1-inch blocks were used to teach color recognition, naming, number concepts, and position concepts such as up, down, behind, beneath, before, in front of, and so on. In addition, graded series of block designs, including three-dimensional constructions, were copied and even transformed (the child copied with red and green blocks an intricate design composed of blue and yellow blocks).

Because the children initially showed little categorizing ability, training in concept formation began with concepts already familiar to the child or ones that could be easily learned. Then by guidance in classification, generalization, and reclassification, hierarchies of concepts were established. For example, to a group composed of a red, a green, and a yellow apple, a pear and a peach were added for the label fruit. Then beans were added to expand the category to plants;

cheese was added to extend it to all foods; and finally clothing was added to teach "necessities of life." As the children's ability developed, they were encouraged to exercise it outside the schoolroom. The supermarket, for example, held unlimited possibilities for categorizing, generalizing, and reclassifying.

Along with this training the teacher continuously encouraged the development of attitudes and motives necessary for school learning—persistence; achievement motivation; delay of gratification; and interest in books, crayons, pencils, and school materials.

The summer school sessions were only half the program. During the winter months a weekly home visit was made by a certified elementary school teacher. She explained the program to the mother and showed her how to stimulate cognitive and language growth during regular domestic activities—for example, by describing and explaining the function of peeling potatoes or of planning the family meals. The home visitor brought books and suggested that the mother read to the child, discuss pictures, and present simple demonstrations. She also arranged to have the mother visit the nursery school during the summer session, and she interpreted the activities there.

At the end of the 3-year program, the youngsters scored 9 IQ points higher than a matched control group who had been followed during the entire period but lived 60 miles away and so had no contact with the project. Both groups were again tested in 1968, at the end of their fourth grade in elementary school; this was *3 years after the training had terminated.* Although the IQ in both groups had dropped somewhat, the children from the experimental program *retained* a 9-IQ-point advantage over the controls. Klaus and Gray concluded that while the impact of the program was not lost, continued intervention would be necessary to offset the effects of a low-income home background.

There were some interesting sidelights to the experiment. First, the test performance of the younger siblings of children who attended the nursery school was superior to that of the siblings of the control group. Evidently the mothers' improved child-rearing practices had a broad effect. Second, the effect of the program, including the home visits, diffused to other households in the ghetto community. A matched sample of neighborhood children scored higher in IQ than the control sample who lived 60 miles away.

CARL BEREITER AND SIEGFRIED ENGELMANN, UNIVERSITY OF ILLINOIS

The preschool training programs that followed Klaus and Gray's project have tended to differ from it in two respects: first, in extending the classroom instruction over the entire academic year rather than confining it to the summer; and second, in focusing more heavily on academic material as the context for teaching thinking skills. Bereiter and Engelmann's preschool program illustrates this.

The Bereiter-Engelmann approach took its start from an examination of what a preschool should accomplish for poverty children. Poverty children fail to advance normally in elementary school. Instead, their relative scores on standardized achievement tests of reading and arithmetic show a steady decline with age. Bereiter and Engelmann saw this as the result not of a lack of fundamental learning capacity, but rather of a lack of learning. Specifically, children from a low-income home environment fail to develop the concepts and skills that are prerequisites for school success. On intelligence tests, these deficiencies show up as poor scores in language ability (vocabulary size, sentence length) and in reasoning or logical development.

Some preschools start with the notion that children from low-income families have been subject to sensory deprivation —a lack of stimulation. And so these schools try to compress an "enriched" middle-class childhood into 9 months. The children are surrounded with toys, materials for handicrafts, and so on. But Bereiter and Engelmann noted that there is really no lack of sensory stimulation in the ghetto—radios and phonographs play, people are ever present. In fact, in some cases, the noise and constant commotion of overcrowded living conditions may cause the child to tune out his attention in a way that is detrimental to school learning. What the lower-class child lacks is not sensory stimulation, but experiences that have definite educational value and that lay the groundwork for further academic growth. This is more properly regarded as *cultural deprivation* (referring to a specific technological-literate *culture*) than as sensory deprivation, and it is highlighted by the verbal interactions characteristic of low-income homes. Communications consist largely of demands, commands, venting of feelings, expressions of wants, and sharing of experiences. But the child has few verbal interactions with an adult in which knowledge is presented and in which language is used to inquire, analyze, explain, and deduce. It is experiences of this sort that nurture extensive and precise language growth, as well as accurate analytical thinking. (Klaus and Gray also noted that the poverty home's "restrictive language code" retards the development of both language and thinking skills.)

The reasoning deficiency of poverty children is manifested in several ways. For example, Bereiter and Engelmann characterized these children's mental processing as one-shot thinking. Their background has not taught them to perform conceptual operations—to compare, combine, and translate. They have not developed the technique of internal dialogue, whereby they ask themselves questions—"Is this true?" "Does it have that characteristic?"—in proceeding through a step-by-step sequence of deductions. Thus they can easily memorize the rule: "If it has a beginning and an ending it is a word." Yet even after learning to identify beginnings and endings, they cannot consistently apply this simple rule. They are not in the habit of systematically taking the question "Is it a word?" and breaking it into the subquestions "Does it have a beginning?" "Does it have an ending?" "Did I answer yes to both questions?"

If the answer to a problem is not immediately available, if it requires any complexities of thought, it is inaccessible. In fact, Bereiter and Engelmann reported that the children believe the answer to a question *should* be given immediately, rather than after a certain amount of thinking.

A characteristic lack of interest in cognitive growth is also observed among children from low-income families. Culturally advantaged children are concerned about gaps or inconsistencies in their understanding and are eager to learn and improve their ability to solve problems. But poverty children show little drive to acquire intellectual skills and knowledge. This naturally adds to their difficulties when they enter elementary school.

The Bereiter-Engelmann preschool program set itself two objectives: first, to develop facility in basic patterns of reasoning such as *if-then* and *either-or;* and second, to teach primary topics of academic knowledge such as the alphabet and counting. The program listed 15 specific "minimum goals":

> 1. Ability to use both affirmative and *not* statements in reply to the question "What is this?" "This is a ball. This is not a book."
>
> 2. Ability to use both affirmative and *not* statements in response to the command "Tell me about this_____[ball, pencil, etc.]." "This pencil is red. This pencil is not blue."
>
> 3. Ability to handle polar opposites ("If it is not_____, it must be_____") for at least four concept pairs, e.g., big-little, up-down, long-short, fat-skinny.
>
> 4. Ability to use the following prepositions correctly in statements describing arrangements of objects: on, in, under, over, between. "Where is the pencil?" "The pencil is under the book."
>
> 5. Ability to name positive and negative instances for at

least four classes, such as tools, weapons, pieces of furniture, wild animals, farm animals, and vehicles. "Tell me something that is a weapon." "A gun is a weapon." "Tell me something that is not a weapon." "A cow is not a weapon." The child should also be able to apply these class concepts correctly to nouns with which he is familiar, e.g., "Is a crayon a piece of furniture?" "No, a crayon is not a piece of furniture. A crayon is something to write with."

6. Ability to perform simple *if-then* deductions. The child is presented a diagram containing big squares and little squares. All the big squares are red, but the little squares are of various other colors. "If the square is big, what do you know about it?" "It's red."

7. Ability to use *not* in deductions. "If the square is little, what else do you know about it?" "It is not red."

8. Ability to use *or* in simple deductions. "If the square is little, then it is not red. What else do you know about it?" "It's blue *or* yellow."

9. Ability to name the basic colors, plus white, black, and brown.

10. Ability to count aloud to 20 without help and to 100 with help at decade points (30, 40, etc.).

11. Ability to count objects correctly up to ten.

12. Ability to recognize and name the vowels and at least 15 consonants.

13. Ability to distinguish printed words from pictures.

14. Ability to rhyme in some fashion to produce a word that rhymes with a given word, to tell whether two words do or do not rhyme, or to complete unfamiliar rhyming jingles like "I had a dog, and his name was Abel; I found him hiding under the______."

15. A sight-reading vocabulary of at least four words in addition to proper names, with evidence that the printed word has the same meaning for them as the corresponding spoken word. "What word is this?" "Cat." "Is this a thing that goes 'Woof-woof'?" "No, it goes 'Meow.'"

Overall class size was 15, but 3 teachers were used so that the pupil-teacher ratio was a low 5:1. Each teacher had a specialty: Language (with the emphasis on verbal reasoning rather than just expression), Reading, or Arithmetic. The class was split into three groups and the groups went into separate rooms for instruction in one of the three areas. The groups periodically changed rooms so that each child received instruction in all three areas every day. Teaching sessions were 20 minutes long and were distributed over 2 hours—with intervening periods for lunch, singing, reading, and story discussion.

The teaching format consisted of intensive, repetitive, attention-demanding, highly structured drill. Discipline was strict and pertinent to the task being practiced; errors were pointed out explicitly rather than glossed over in vague terms; and most important, emphatic and overt response was required of each child.

Analytical reasoning and sequential deduction were taught with a variety of problem tasks. For example, a lesson in *if-then* reasoning began by placing five squares on the blackboard—two big white ones, one small white one, and two small red ones. The children then learned to draw correct conclusions of the following type:

> If a square is red, it is______. (little)
> If a square is big, it is______. (white)
> If a square is little, it is______. (white or red)
> If a square is *not* white, it is______. (little)

Subsequently, *if-thens* in everyday situations were demonstrated.

During the lesson, the teacher continually required responses from the children. This ensured that their attention was properly focused on the subject and that they were actively proceeding through the sequential steps of analysis and deduction. Considerable student response is a central feature of all the intellect-training experiments. In the Bereiter and Engelmann program this was accomplished through *unison response,* described as follows:

> As a rule of thumb, the teacher should assume that while she is working with one child individually, the others in the class are not learning anything. Accordingly, she should work with children individually no more than is absolutely necessary. She can avoid individual sessions by introducing unison responses. In a sense, a unison response enables the teacher to work individually with each member of the class throughout the entire period. In another sense, it allows her to work with the entire group, so that the total number of responses produced during a class period is increased many times, and the speed with which concepts are learned is generally increased accordingly. The deprived child's mastery of many fundamental concepts is premised on a certain amount of practice, and the practice is as effective in unison as it is individually.

Disadvantaged children have a tendency to guess answers rather than think. They may answer yes to "Do you know . . ." before the remainder of the question is completed. The experienced teacher should be sensitive to this and try to counteract it:

> If the task requires the child to make a visual discrimination and the child has not inspected the material, the teacher can assume that the child is about to make a guessed response. She can prevent it by saying "Now look at it. What is this? What do you know about it?"
>
> If the task requires several steps in reasoning but the child begins to respond immediately, the teacher can assume the child could not have gone through the reasoning process. She can prevent a guess by saying "Now think. Take it a step at a time. What do you ask yourself first?"

Bereiter and Engelmann's book, *Teaching Disadvantaged Children in the Preschool,* is indispensable reading for those interested in the cognitive deficiences of poverty children. The book presents a full picture of their learning difficulties, along with a detailed description of the remedial program.

While specific content material in arithmetic and reading was taught in the respective classes, the major emphasis of the program was on teaching overall thinking ability and language skill. Appendix 2 gives a sample of the program.

The Bereiter-Engelmann program has been criticized by some developmental psychologists as being too specialized and failing to deal with the whole child, including his personality, social growth, and total education. To this, Bereiter and Engelmann have answered that it is a question of time and priorities; the slum child must acquire in 1 year skills and concepts that the middle-class youngster has had several years to develop. For example, when the choice is either a field trip where the child can experience the look, smell, and feel of sheep, or extra hours spent teaching the child to understand the use of *if-then, or, not,* and similar relational words, the latter seems of more immediate importance.

But there is yet another consideration. The type of nursery school that is best suited to meet the social growth needs of middle-class children is the one that balances with their home experiences. Such a school allows greater amounts of physical freedom, peer contact, nonverbal experience, present rather than future orientation, noncompetitiveness, myth, and pretense. But the lower-class home already includes sufficient experience of this sort. The lower-class child attains a balanced and total development through training in academically pertinent attitudes, orientations, and thinking skills.

Children who attended the Bereiter-Engelmann preschool for the normal academic year showed marked improvement in many scholastically relevant measures. For one thing, they were prepared with an appropriate attitude for elementary school learning. When they entered the preschool, they were intellectually apathetic and had to be continually coaxed to think, to try hard, to pay attention. By the time they left, learning was a challenge. They needed merely to be told that a problem was difficult, that they would probably have trouble solving it, and they were readily motivated to try to figure it out.

More concrete evidence, however, is seen in gains on objective test scores. On standard achievement tests of reading and arithmetic, the children averaged over a year above the national norms for their age group. Without the preschool intervention, such children would have scored below the mean for their age group, indicating that most of them would face serious academic handicaps. Furthermore, Bereiter has reported that in four recent replications of the program, IQ gains have averaged 15 points. Thus, significant increases in both specific academic skills and general thinking capacity have been achieved through direct, intensive training.

MERLE B. KARNES, UNIVERSITY OF ILLINOIS

Karnes and her associates have conducted a series of studies comparing different types of preschool programs.

One study showed that a preschool intensive training program was more effective than a traditional "free-play" or Montessori-type nursery school in reversing the IQ deficit shown by children of poverty. The intensive training program resembled those of Klaus and Gray and of Bereiter and Engelmann in general orientation, but it also incorporated certain differences. The full reports (cited in the bibliography) give specific details. A 5:1 student-teacher ratio was used and the program emphasized verbal interaction and continuous response from the children. It centered on 20-minute learning periods in three areas—Math Concepts, Language Arts and Reading Readiness, and Science-Social Studies.

The children exposed to intensive training gained about 8 points more on the Stanford-Binet IQ test than did those who attended the traditional nursery school or the Montessori school.

Another of Karnes's studies demonstrated that paraprofessionals (properly trained mothers or teenagers) working under the guidance of an experienced teacher were about as effective as certified teachers in an intensive training program for preschoolers. Teenagers, mothers, or certified teachers using the intensive program format produced Stanford-Binet IQ gains of 12 to 14 points over the academic year. Equivalent gains also occurred on the Frostig Developmental Test of Visual Perception, the Metropolitan Number Readiness Test, and the Metropolitan Reading Readiness Test. The professional teachers did, however, appear to be a little more effective in conveying language skills as measured by the Illinois Test of Psycholinguistic Abilities.

This study's primary importance is its demonstration of an economically feasible method for instituting intensive intervention programs, with a low pupil-teacher ratio. In general, Karnes has taken the position, based on research in the area, that intensive training programs for preschoolers have proved their effectiveness. Subsequent experimentation must concern itself with finding optimum formats and with developing possibilities for implementation.

MARION BLANK AND FRANCES SOLOMON, ALBERT EINSTEIN COLLEGE OF MEDICINE

This study is somewhat different from those reviewed so far in that preschoolers were tutored *individually* rather than in small groups, but tutoring was done for only 15 to 20 minutes a day.

Blank and Solomon began with essentially the same observations made by Bereiter and Engelmann. Children from low-income homes exhibit widespread deficiencies ranging across motivational, affective, and cognitive areas. Some compensatory programs (such as Head Start) expose the children to a broad range of stimuli deemed beneficial—toys, trips, various equipment—in attempting to alleviate the deficiencies. Such programs assume that all types of stimulation are equally effective. But what the children really need is training "to organize thoughts, to reflect upon situations, to comprehend the meaning of events, and to structure behavior so as to be able to choose among alternatives." Merely enriching the environment perceptually will not guide the development of this capacity. Clay molding, painting, and such activities may have educational value, but they will not necessarily teach sequential, organized thinking.

One-to-one interaction with an adult, who guides the development of the child's language and thinking abilities, seems to be the critical advantage a middle-class home provides. Blank and Solomon sought to duplicate this for the deprived youngster. They centered their program around such patterns of thought as cause and effect, categorization, foreseeing consequences, and sequential analysis, using a kind of Socratic dialogue to encourage reflective thinking. The preschooler was tutored individually and was drawn into discussions in which he was taught to probe, investigate, and seek information from his own experience. For example, he was taught elementary conceptual categories such as food, clothing, transportation, and job function. Then, perhaps after feeding a doll an imaginary apple, the child was asked what other *fruit* the doll might eat. And a second step in conceptual thinking was introduced with questions requiring category exclusion, such as "What are some foods that are *not* fruits?"

Cause-and-effect reasoning was stimulated through questions like "Why can't we go out and play in the rain?" "Where is the rain coming from?" Sustained sequential thinking and foreseeing consequences were furthered by simple experiments involving change of material substance. In experimenting with vegetable dyes, first the functions and characteristics of the dyes were discussed. Then the student was asked to consider what would happen under various circumstances, such as leaving the dye in concentrated form or diluting it with water. In each case the child carried out the necessary operations in order to experience the words and ideas that coordinated directly with sequential cause-and-effect change.

The training format did not center exclusively on verbal responses—sometimes actions were called for. But carrying out the actions required comprehending and thinking about the situation. For example, the child might be given a group of different colored blocks and asked to select "two red blocks and one green block." Thus, instead of responding to the primitive sensation of color alone, he compared objects and made decisions within the confines of number concept. As a second example, the child might be asked to draw something. After drawing a circle, he might be asked to draw something "other than a circle." In this task, the child was required to categorize forms and then operate under the conditions of exclusion, rather than drawing aimlessly and spontaneously.

Blank and Solomon conducted their study with 4-year-old youngsters attending a traditional (free-play) nursery school in a socioeconomically depressed area of New York City. For the special one-to-one tutoring, selected children were taken to a small room, separate from the main classroom of the nursery school. Several groups were used.

In one group each child was tutored individually for 15 to 20 minutes a day, 5 days a week over several months. The Stanford-Binet IQ of this group increased from 97.7 to 112.2 —a gain of 14.5 points.

A second group was tutored the same way, but only 3 days a week. The average IQ gain of these children was 7 points.

A third group served as an untutored control. Each of these children met with the same teacher for an individual session 15 to 20 minutes a day 5 days a week, but he was not tutored. He was exposed to identical materials but was permitted to engage in activities of his own choice. IQ for these children improved only 2 points.

For still another comparison, the IQs of children who did not participate in the experimental program in any way were also measured. These children merely attended the regular nursery school from which the tutored children were randomly selected. The school provided no special training in thinking skills. Average IQ in this group increased 1.3 points.

This experiment indicates that a relatively small amount of individual instruction, teaching the child how to think actively and thoroughly, goes a long way in breeding intelligence. In fact, it suggests that busing and other methods for integrating schools should be supplemented by some form of specific cognitive therapy, since dialogue focusing on cause and effect, reasons for action, thorough analysis, etc. may be the decisive component of middle-class home stimulation. Future research may investigate the relative advantages of one-to-one training as contrasted with the unison response method of Bereiter and Engelmann. But Blank and Solomon did point out the feasibility of wide-scale one-to-one training:

> Although most educators acknowledge that ideal teaching would be a one-to-one relation, this has been deemed impractical because of the costs involved. The conclusion of excessive costs is based on the implicit assumption that individual teaching would or should occupy most of the teaching day. Little consideration has been given to the possible effectiveness of short periods of daily individual instruction, even though such instruction is widely and effectively used in the initial teaching of language to other language-deficient groups, such as deaf children.

In conclusion, Blank and Solomon recommended that a program of their type should probably be continued for 2 or 3 years to ensure that gains in thinking capacity would be maintained independently by the child.

JEROME KAGAN, HARVARD UNIVERSITY

In the experiments described so far, children of between 3 and 5 years of age were trained in thinking skills—and the training appears to have been highly effective. In one study, reviewed on pages 42–47, intervention commenced much earlier—shortly after birth—and the gains were dramatic. Undoubtedly, the earlier an optimum environment is provided to the child, the better.

However, let us stop to consider an important theoretical question regarding the development of intelligence. Some psychologists have feared that the first year of a child's life has a crucial and irreversible effect on his later mental ability; that is, if a child does not receive sufficient and proper stimulation during infancy, his normal intellectual growth—perhaps the maturation of complex neural networks—is permanently stunted. Fortunately, as Jerome Kagan has shown, this is not the case.

Several societies around the world make a regular practice of raising infants under what might be considered conditions of extreme sensory deprivation. Kagan studied a village of Guatemalan Indians whose infants are kept in dark huts. During the first year of their lives the infants are not played with or even talked to. This is done to protect them from disease. As a result, at the age of 2 years the youngsters are severely retarded in motor and mental development, and they score very low on standardized tests of infant ability. But the retardation is not permanent. Kagan tested older children, 5 to 11 years of age, from the same village and found that their primary mental abilities are basically equal to those of American children. Their scores on tests of memory, perceptual analysis, and ability to reason and draw inferences from pictures or orally presented material are perfectly normal.

Kagan also noted that this type of restricted infantile environment is characteristic of middle-class families living in eastern Holland. Infants are placed in rooms with little adult contact and no toys (again for fear of disease) until they are a year old. But by 5 years these children too are mentally normal.

In his concluding remarks, Kagan warned that American education tends to give up too quickly with slum children whose reading, writing, and arithmetic are below standard:

> All children—except perhaps the approximately 7% born with some brain damage due either to heredity, disease during pregnancy, or difficulty during birth—have the capacity for basic intellectual functions, including the ability to understand and speak a language, to think symbolically, to place events into conceptual groups, to infer complex relations between events, to deduce implications, to analyze the environment into parts and wholes, and to remember large chunks of past experience.

Kagan recommended that methods be used to break the circle of defeatism and bring the benefits of the educational system to all youngsters, including the children of poverty. The techniques developed by Klaus and Gray, Bereiter and Engelmann, Karnes, Solomon and Blank, and others may be one way to help achieve this end.

THE MILWAUKEE PROJECT, UNIVERSITY OF WISCONSIN*

The Milwaukee Project, under the directorship of Rick Heber, was begun by an interdisciplinary team from education, psychology, psychiatry, speech therapy, and sociology. It is probably the most lengthy and comprehensive study ever undertaken on training intelligence, and it has also achieved the most dramatic gains in IQ. This is in itself highly significant. It demonstrates that the benefits of IQ training are di-

*The official title of this project is Rehabilitation of Families at Risk for Mental Retardation. The present summary is based partly on the most recent project progress report and partly on a review article by S. Strickland (see Bibliography).

rectly related to the amount of training undertaken—which is exactly what we should expect if intelligence is basically a learned capacity.

In 1964 the Wisconsin team began to explore the fact that by some estimates 6 million Americans are mentally retarded, although about 80 percent of these persons display no identifiable gross pathology of the central nervous system. Furthermore, such cases of *functional retardation* (illiteracy and extremely low IQ without signs of neural pathology) occur mainly in economically depressed areas.

The researchers first surveyed the IQ of schoolchildren in a section of Milwaukee that had the lowest family income, poorest housing, and highest index of overcrowding—a veritable slum. Maternal IQ was isolated as a factor of primary importance. Although fewer than one half of the mothers in the study had IQs below 80, they accounted for four fifths of the children in the survey with such low IQs. Furthermore, the lower a mother's IQ, the lower her child's IQ tended to be. Father's intelligence was not focused on as sharply by researchers, since often the father did not reside in the home.

Repeated home visits made by the team of researchers convinced them that there was no reason to conclude that the family's retardation was hereditary. Instead, they observed that retarded mothers create a social environment—much like that described by Klaus and Gray—that is distinct from their neighbors and that appears to be responsible for the perpetuation of low intelligence.

In 1966 the Infant Education Center was established to see whether this slum-related form of mental retardation could be prevented. A group of 40 mothers with IQs of less than 75 participated on a voluntary basis. The newborn infants of one half of these mothers were selected for the experimental program, while the remainder served as a control group. A teacher visited each infant in the experimental group for several hours each day, from shortly after the baby was brought home from the hospital until he was about 3 months old. After that, the mother took the child to the center. Each child received a wide variety of stimulation (designed to develop perceptual-motor and language-cognitive abilities) from an adult on a one-to-one basis until he was 2 years old. The mother, in turn, was instructed in homemaking and baby-care skills and was given vocational training.

At 2 years of age, the child was placed in a class with 5 other youngsters and 3 teachers; by age 4 years the class size was increased to 8; and at age 5, the class size rose to 11.

Each of the three teachers in a class had a specialty area —Language Development and Expression, Reading, or Mathematics/Problem Solving. The teachers were not necessarily college graduates, but all underwent an 8-month training period.

On 4 days of the week a definite schedule was followed. The children arrived at 9 o'clock and ate breakfast. At 9:30 the class split into three groups with each teacher instructing her special area. Each teaching period lasted 30 minutes. The first 20 minutes consisted of structured training and guidance using standard equipment, such as the Peabody Language Development Kit, as well as special materials and methods developed for the project. During the final 10 minutes, each child could continue with the activity started by the teacher or proceed to use the instructional materials in any way he pleased. Basically the training was similar to that used by Bereiter and Engelmann and other researchers whose programs have already been described. However, the smaller student-teacher ratio and greater amount of teaching time (in terms both of hours per day and duration of the program) allowed more personal attention, a broader range of thinking exercises and academic topics, and a less structured pace.

The group switched teachers (and instructional areas) at half-hour intervals. A 30-minute free-play period was scheduled between the second and third classes, so that the third class ended at 11:30, at which time the children either watched "Sesame Street" or continued in activities begun earlier.

After lunch and a nap, the youngsters separated to attend two more classes in the afternoon—one a language class that emphasized communication and problem solving, and the other a general topics class covering art, science, and music. While two teachers were occupied with these classes, the third teacher worked individually with any student who needed special help in some subject.

The children were tested regularly to evaluate the effects of the training. On various measures of academic and cognitive abilities, the experimental group greatly outscored the control group, who, for comparison purposes, had not been included in the training program but had been left to mature in the slum environment. For example, one measure used was the Bellugi-Klima Test of Grammatical Comprehension, which evaluates the child's ability to comprehend 16 progressively more difficult verbal forms (e.g., sentences involving active versus passive voice; conjuctions—*and/or, either/neither;* adjectival modifiers; comparatives). On this test, the untrained control group lagged 1 to 2 years behind the experimental group (testing was periodically conducted when the children were between 3 and 5 years old). Similarly, when both groups were tested at age 4 years 7 months on the Illinois Test of Psycholinguistic Abilities (a reliable predictor of reading readiness), the experimental group's mean score was equivalent to the national norm for children aged 5 years 3 months, whereas the control group's mean was at the national norm for children aged only 3 years 10 months.

Figure 1 presents the mean IQ scores made at successive age levels by the control group, the experimental group, and the older siblings of the children in the experimental group. The older siblings of the experimental group children had not participated in the training program, but were tested for the purpose of making long-term comparisons.

The controls and the older siblings showed the gradual

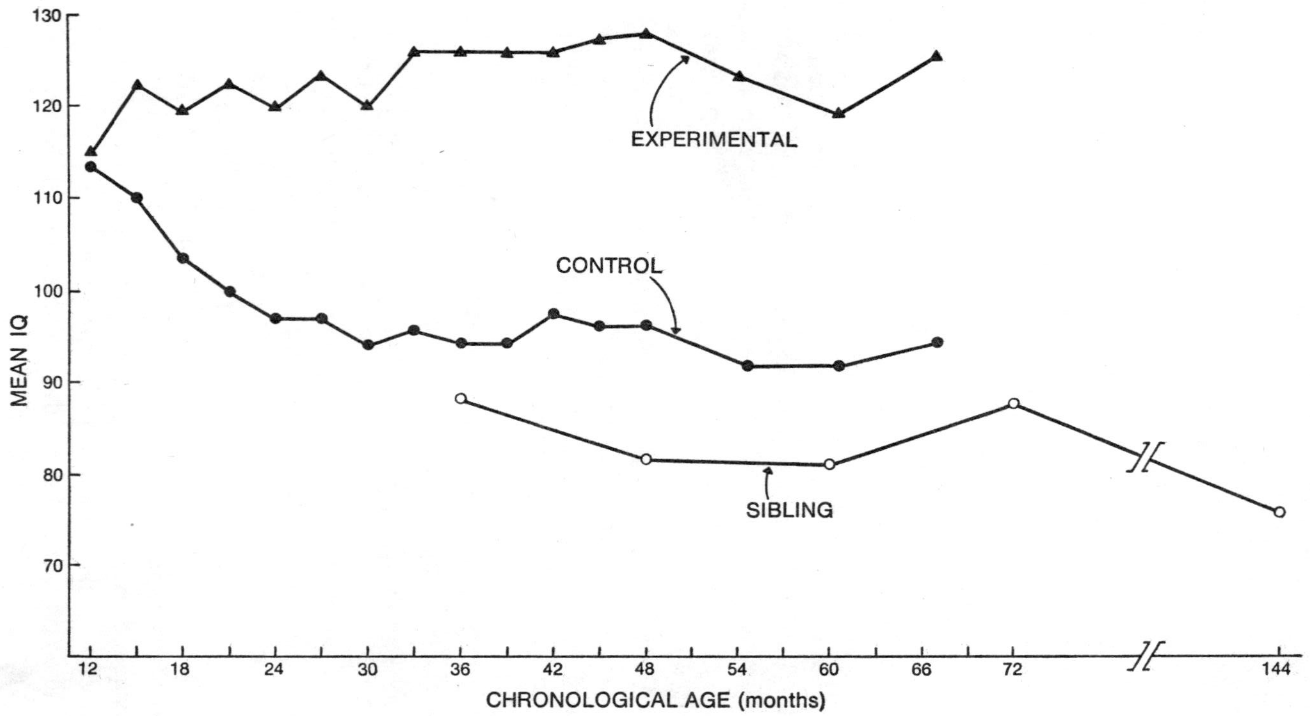

Figure 1. Mean IQ Performance with Increasing Age for the Experimental and Control Groups in the Milwaukee Project

IQ decline that is characteristic of poverty children. By contrast, the mean IQ of the experimental group was well above the national norm. At the most recent testing point, 66 months, the mean IQ of the experimental group was 124, whereas the control group's mean was 94. In fact, some of the experimental children registered IQs as high as 135—especially remarkable when contrasted with their mothers' IQs of less than 75.

In an article in the *Educational Researcher,* Ellis Page, of the University of Connecticut, outlined what he considered to be methodological complications in the Milwaukee project. Page's points are technical and detailed, so they will not be discussed here. The interested reader may want to read Page's article to see the types of problems that must be considered in preschool training research. Recognizing such problems, Heber has been reserved in predicting just how successful the compensatory program will be in affecting long-term behavior. The Wisconsin group will continue to collect test data on the children for a number of years. Heber has pointed out, however, that it is hard to imagine these children ever backsliding to the level of academic deficiency typical of children raised in poverty homes by mothers with low IQs.

DOES PRESCHOOL TRAINING COMPLETELY COMPENSATE THE POVERTY CHILD?

Two recent "Hyman Blumberg Symposia on Research in Early Childhood Education" held at The Johns Hopkins University brought together the nation's leading experts in preschool education for disadvantaged youngsters. (The reports from the symposia have been published in two books, edited by Julian C. Stanley.) The recurrent theme and overall conclusion of both symposia was that a properly structured preschool has very powerful effects on the academic skills of disadvantaged youngsters, but that gradually the gains may fade if the educational system does not follow through in supporting the continued intellectual growth of children from poverty homes.

Much additional research is needed on the problem. The remainder of this chapter summarizes studies concerned with training thinking skills in older students. These studies offer important suggestions for programs designed to follow through on preschool gains. In fact, researchers may find that special training provided to more mature students has an unexpectedly strong influence on their subsequent academic performance, since the motivations and day-to-day experiences of older students are less restricted by and tied to their home backgrounds. As educational researcher David Ausubel has pointed out, there is no theoretical reason to assume that cognitive training cannot be profitably undertaken with older students.

JOSEPH MARRON, U.S. MILITARY ACADEMY, WEST POINT*

In 1965, Joseph Marron, of the Office of the Director of Admissions and Registrar, U.S. Military Academy, West Point, conducted a study to determine whether full-time preparatory schools that specialize in raising Scholastic Aptitude Test (SAT) scores actually get results. Such prep schools are attended by high school graduates whose SAT scores bar them from admission to the colleges of their choice. An official of the College Entrance Examination Board with whom I spoke reported that universities sometimes send promising athletes to such prep schools to help them meet the university's admission requirements. Furthermore, some of the prep schools are run by the three branches of the armed services. Thus, for example, Air Force enlisted men who show good

*I am indebted to Dr. Lloyd Humphreys, of the University of Illinois, for bringing this study to my attention.

service qualifications but poor academic aptitude may be sent to the Air Force Preparatory School before entering the Air Force Academy.

Marron pointed out that the coaching programs evaluated earlier by the Educational Testing Service and the College Entrance Examination Board had been limited to one or two hours of practice a week over several months. These evaluations (one of which is summarized in Chapter II) showed that coaching produced no appreciable effect on test scores. But the question whether full-time course work aimed at improving test scores was effective had not been systematically investigated.

At 10 prep schools across the country, the SAT was administered at the beginning of the term in September and then again in March. The 10 schools were:

The Boyden School; San Diego, California
Braden's; Cornwall, New York
Bullis School; Silver Spring, Maryland
Columbian Preparatory School; Washington, D.C.
Millard School; Bandon, Oregon
Northwestern Prep; Minneapolis, Minnesota
Sullivan School; Washington, D.C.
U.S. Air Force Preparatory School; Colorado Springs, Colorado
U.S. Military Academy Preparatory School; Fort Belvoir, Virginia
U.S. Naval Academy Preparatory School; Bainbridge, Maryland

Among the schools, 714 students were involved in the research.

The results of the study were clear: Prep school training had a significant effect on SAT scores. Scores on the SAT Verbal Aptitude Section increased an average of 57 points, and those on the SAT Mathematics Aptitude Section increased 79 points. This is an overall average increase of 136 points on the SAT, brought about through roughly 6 months of intensive training.

In addition to the main experiment, a small study was conducted to determine whether simply taking the SAT several times was responsible for the improvement. It was not—the test score increases were directly attributable to the training.

Marron carried the study further and asked a second question: Had the training merely inflated test scores, or did the training actually improve academic learning capacity? Since, as noted earlier, the SAT is composed of reading comprehension, verbal reasoning, and mathematical reasoning problems, it is high in what psychometrists call *content validity.* In other words, its content closely parallels the actual activities (reading difficult text and reasoning) that are called into play in college courses. Therefore we should expect an SAT score increase to be accompanied by at least some degree of improved academic performance.

Sufficient data to test this question were available for only 6 of the 10 prep schools. Graduates of these schools were followed through the end of the freshman year of college, at which time their class rankings were computed.

The college grades of students from 4 of the 6 prep schools were fully up to the level of their improved SAT scores. Apparently the training had not artificially boosted test scores, but had produced a true change in educational potential. For the students from the remaining 2 prep schools, course grades were not entirely commensurate with SAT performance. Whether there had been at least a partial improvement in academic aptitude was not clear from the study. Marron, in pointing out the limitations of his experiment, mentioned the possibility that academic aptitude may have improved more than the data indicated. But on the basis of the overall results, he cautioned that until more information is known, SAT scores of prep school graduates should be viewed carefully, with an eye toward their true validity.

The data from this study have important implications for public education. High school students registering to take the SAT for college admission are given a booklet that contains the following information:

> *How Should You Prepare for the SAT?*
>
> The most appropriate and practical preparation is to study this booklet, particularly the directions and sample questions beginning on page 6. The College Board suggests that students not invest time and money on special drilling or coaching programs. Time spent on general reading and school assignments will prove at least as beneficial in preparing for the SAT and far more beneficial in preparing for college.

This statement, in combination with the widespread notion that mental capacity is dictated genetically, has given many students an inaccurate picture of their educational promise. They come away with the misconception that there is really no alternative method for them to improve their SAT scores, and that a low score is basically a reflection of lesser mental endowment. The belief is deeply ingrained in modern education. Guidance counselors, academic advisers, teachers, and college testing officers have all interpreted this statement to mean that no effective training methods exist for improving SAT scores. This interpretation is constantly communicated to students.

The College Board's statement is meant to protect students from wasting their money on short-term cram courses that are, in fact, relatively ineffective. But the statement fails to distinguish between drilling cram courses and extensive training, and thus creates the mistaken impression that no training is effective. The Marron study was financially supported by a grant from the College Board—the board was interested in whether prep school training affects college admission decisions involving SAT scores. Thus, the College Board knew of the West Point study back in 1965. Yet the study has never been reported in the professional literature, nor is it cited in the various booklets and bulletins about the SAT that the College Board publishes and distributes. This oversight has serious implications, for the Marron study calls into question the supposed immutability of mental tests such as the SAT, an assumption that is a mainstay of hereditarians, who argue that intelligence is primarily genetic and cannot be improved through training. Any demonstration of large gains on test scores brought about through training is extremely damaging to the hereditarian position—and is a step in the direction of educational progress.

The College Board's statement that "time spent on general reading and school assignments" is effective preparation is true enough for those who have mastered the skills of good comprehension and academic study. But many students, especially those from low-income homes, have not learned *how* to comprehend, analyze, and integrate academic material. They have gone through conventional education and have benefited minimally. They would reap the greatest profit from a training program that develops their scholastic learning ability. Yet the belief that academic intelligence is untrainable has been a major deterrent to the establishment of "academic skills courses" throughout the educational system. Content courses are taught, but courses that teach the student *how* to deal with reasoning problems and with complex verbal materials are missing.

In Chapter II, psychologist Ernest Hilgard is quoted as noting that communication gaps between the various branches of psychology and education have acted to hinder research on intelligence. This is illustrated, to some degree, by the West Point study. For example, consider the following questions: What were the training methods used by the prep schools? Why did some schools appear to be more effective than others in actually improving academic aptitude? What were the student-teacher ratios? Was individual tutoring periodically used? One suspects that prep schools employ small classes and extensive student involvement—much like the preschool programs of Bereiter and Engelmann, Heber, and others. But these questions were not answered in the West Point report. Psychometrists, who sponsored and conducted the study, were, understandably, not able to explore these topics. Their main concern was whether training reduced the validity of the SAT (that is, whether it reduced the SAT's effectiveness in predicting college grades). But educators, who could have used detailed information on training methods in implementing special programs throughout their own school systems, have been left uninformed about how effective prep school programs really are. A thorough study of the prep school training procedures might contribute significantly to the science of teaching academic intelligence.

BENJAMIN BLOOM AND LOIS BRODER, UNIVERSITY OF CHICAGO

A quarter of a century ago, Bloom and Broder reported a study that should have served as a model for a new wave of research in training mental ability. The time, however, was not ripe. Bloom and Broder's approach ran contrary to the existing traditions of American psychology. Moreover, when the study was conducted (1945 to 1950) the question of whether academic aptitude could be improved through special training had not yet become a focus of national concern.

Bloom and Broder's study had two parts. First, a thorough analysis was made of the mental activities characterizing college students with high and low academic aptitudes. Then, based on these results, a remedial program was developed for training academic thinking ability. The remedial program was tested in a pilot experiment and proved highly successful.

To begin with, college students with low scores on academic aptitude examinations were tested individually on a series of academic reasoning problems. They were asked to think aloud or introspect while solving the problems so that their thinking activities could be monitored. A contrast group of students with high academic aptitude scores was also tested in this manner. They too reported introspectively—fully describing their thoughts and their methods of solution—while attempting to solve the same series of problems.

Although some of the problems employed in the experiment were more difficult and required knowledge of specific academic topics, the questions were generally similar to the following:

> DIRECTIONS: In each of the following items, you are given statements and four conclusions. Assume that the statements are true. You are to judge which of the conclusions then logically follows; i.e., must be true if the statements are true. Blacken the answer space corresponding to the one conclusion which logically follows. If none of the conclusions logically follows, blacken answer space E.
>
> STATEMENT:
>
> Any action that impedes the war effort of the United States should be made illegal.
>
> All strikes impede the war effort of the United States.
>
> CONCLUSIONS:
>
> A —All strikes should be made illegal.
> B —Some restrictions should be placed on the right to strike but it would be unwise to make them all illegal.
> C —Some strikes should be made illegal.
> D—Unjustifiable strikes should be made illegal.
> E —None of the foregoing conclusions follows.

Bloom and Broder found that each student showed a definite consistency in the way he approached and solved the various problems. This consistency was of such magnitude that

Bloom and Broder regarded it as the student's "habitual" mode of thinking. Furthermore, the habitual problem-solving behavior of low-aptitude college students was characteristically different from that of high-aptitude students. And what is most interesting, this difference corresponds strongly to the contrasting mental habits of low- and high-aptitude *preschoolers* —as described, for example, by Bereiter and Engelmann.

The cognitive profile of low-aptitude college students (as with preschoolers) has two prominent features—features that are, in a sense, mirror images of each other. First, there is one-shot thinking rather than extended, sequential construction of understanding; and second, there is a willingness to allow gaps of knowledge to exist—in effect, an attitude of indifference toward achieving an accurate and complete comprehension of situations and relations.

Bloom and Broder observed that low-aptitude students were mentally careless and superficial in solving problems. They often rushed through the instructions, or even skipped them, and selected a wrong answer because they failed to comprehend what was required. When asked to reread the instructions more carefully, frequently they understood them and proceeded correctly. However, typically they did not peruse the instructions thoroughly on their own, but were satisfied with an incomplete understanding.

In actual problem solving, low-aptitude students were almost completely passive in their thinking. They spent little time considering a question, but chose an answer on the basis of a few clues. Frequently the selection was founded on simply a feeling, an impression, or a guess. High-aptitude students, by contrast, made a decidedly active attack on problems. When a question was initially unclear, they often employed a lengthy sequential analysis in arriving at an answer. They began with what they understood of the problem, drew on other information in their possession to clarify the question further, and carefully proceeded through a chain of steps that finally brought them to a solution.

Closely related to the superficial and careless thinking of low-aptitude students was their inability to take an objective view of a question—a tendency for their subjective opinions to intrude on purely logical considerations. For example, on the problem given above a student chose alternative B and reported: "That would be not only logic, but using my interpretation of equity."

Quite significantly, low-aptitude students tended to place little value on reasoning as a method of solving problems. They did not see problems as susceptible to analysis. Their orientation was not to attack a complex problem by breaking it down into subproblems: Either they knew the answer to a problem or they didn't; and if they didn't they made a cursory evaluation and then guessed.

Having thus isolated the habitual thinking deficiencies of low-aptitude students, Bloom and Broder undertook to develop a remedial training program. This was only a pilot project, but the method they developed may find wide application.

A set of problems was selected on which the contrasting approaches of good and poor students were clearly evident. Introspective reports of extremely capable students were then collected, and these model solutions served as the primary teaching materials.

The actual training was conducted with underachieving university students who volunteered for the remedial program. Training was carried out on an individual basis.

During the first two sessions the trainee was familiarized with the procedure. It was explained that problem solving is a skill, much like tennis or golf, and that the remedial program was designed to teach this skill. It was further emphasized that simply knowing the skill is not sufficient, that a great deal of practice is necessary. In addition, as in tennis, much effort and motivation are required for outstanding performance: A half-hearted attempt does not return the ball to the other end of the tennis court and does not help in attacking and comprehending difficult reasoning problems. Finally, the student was told that his habits of thinking had developed over a long time, from various experiences, and that he was probably, to a degree, unaware of how he solved problems. In the training, his problem-solving methods would be compared with those of consistently successful model students, and he was to regard these comparisons as he would the comparison between a novice and a champion tennis player. In this way, he would learn how to improve his own analytical thinking. After this introduction, the student was instructed in the procedure of verbalizing or thinking aloud while solving sample reasoning problems.

Training began in the third session. The student attempted to solve a problem while thinking aloud, his verbalized solution was reviewed and discussed, and then the protocol of a model's solution to the problem was read. Subsequently, the student was asked to make a list of the differences between his solution and that of the model. At first this was difficult, and the instructor helped by pointing out the contrasts and similarities between the trainee's solution and the model's solution. The instructor emphasized that the student should look for differences that occurred regularly—across a number of problems—rather than those that were unique to individual problems. In a short time the student was able to compile satisfactorily a list of the differences between his solution and the model's solution to a problem.

In the sessions that followed, the time was divided between practice in acquiring the approach used by the model and comparison and analysis of solution protocols. During practice, the student thought aloud as he solved problems, he frequently referred to the list he had made of differences between his methods and the model's, and he tried to apply general principles derived from the list. The trainer continually reminded him to evaluate his approach and to consider the steps he thought the model would take to solve the problem at hand.

Bloom and Broder noted that, initially, low-aptitude students were primarily interested in *what* the right answer to a question was, rather than *how* it was obtained. They saw this as, first, a personality characteristic of poor problem solvers, and second, the product of an educational system that does not emphasize the processes of thinking. Gradually, the students learned to focus on the mental activities and steps leading to a solution.

No standardized tests of academic aptitude or IQ were used in evaluating the effects of the training. Bloom and Broder's primary interest was raising academic achievement through the improvement of thinking skills, and so scholastic grades were taken as the criterion of gain. Comparison with various control groups indicated that grades on comprehensive examinations did increase to a statistically significant degree. The grade increases were such as to allow these students, who had originally been failing and on probation, to continue in college. Marked changes in academic performance were also reported by professors in whose courses the students were registered. Further evidence of improvement was seen in the alteration of problem-solving methods that occurred over the course of the training sessions. The students read instructions more carefully, making a directed effort to understand them completely. They approached problems more actively—they began with what they understood, set up hypotheses, reasoned sequentially in steps, and so on. In addition, students noted carryover effects to all their thinking. For instance, they reported taking a more analytical approach to the arguments of others and "thinking twice" before interjecting comments in class discussion.

Following the success of this experiment, Bloom and Broder ran another small study to explore the possibility of training students in groups rather than individually. The classes varied in size between 5 and 20 students. First, the procedure of analyzing the differences between a model's solution and the student's approach was introduced. In the group sessions, a problem was projected on the screen, and several students were asked to think aloud while solving it. The group members then discussed and compared their approaches. Following this, the model's method was presented, and the students contrasted their approaches with the model's. For this experiment a checklist was developed that listed the major differences between good and poor problem solvers, and each trainee tallied the items on which his technique differed from that of the model's.

Beginning with the third session, students practiced in pairs or in small groups. One student solved a problem while thinking aloud; the others observed and compared his attack with how they believed the model might approach the problem. Students alternated in this procedure and continually tried to learn the model's approach.

In summarizing this study, Bloom and Broder concluded that more could be accomplished with individual training than with group sessions. In one-to-one tutoring the trainee is constantly active in problem solving, and furthermore, the instructor can point out the trainee's specific difficulties. Nevertheless, significant grade improvements did occur following the group experiment. Students who participated in 10 to 12 training sessions made the largest gains. Those who came to only 7 to 9 sessions showed smaller increases. And those who attended fewer than 7 sessions made little or no improvement. Thus, magnitude of improvement was directly related to amount of training.

Bloom and Broder's remedial program was admittedly only a pilot experiment. However, results of their study supply a picture of low academic aptitude that agrees with and adds to that painted by other researchers. In the same vein, their remedial procedure is congruent in principle with the methods devised by Bereiter and Engelmann, Solomon and Blank, and other experimenters. Bloom and Broder's unique contribution was to develop a feasible and promising method for training *adult* academic capacity.

JIM HARDY, PERSONNEL DEPARTMENT OF THE CITY OF TULSA

This experiment involved only one trainee and developed outside the academic setting. It contributes an additional dimension to the emerging picture of aptitude training.

In 1968, Jim Hardy, director of personnel testing for Tulsa, was concerned about the racial imbalance of the Tulsa police department. At the time, Tulsa was using the Science Research Associates Adaptability Test (a typical IQ test) for selection of police officers. Hardy decided to run an experiment and tutor a black job applicant who had been raised in Mississippi and who, he felt, had never had a chance to develop his thinking skills.

Hardy met with his student for 60 to 90 minutes at the end of each work day. Although he developed his training procedure independently, it was similar to that used by Blank and Solomon, Bloom and Broder, and other researchers. For example, Hardy presented his student with newspaper articles to read aloud in sections of about three sentences, and had him explain and discuss them fully. Under Hardy's guidance, the student analyzed the organization of the material, the arguments on either side of a controversy, the temporal order of events, the sequence of cause-and-effect steps leading to an outcome, and so on. Hardy taught his student to read carefully, with full attention to relations and precise ideas. He encouraged his student to do all his outside reading in the same analytical manner, and suggested that he discuss what he read with his wife and explain the articles to her.

Intelligence test items, both verbal and nonverbal, were also used for training—although, of course, none of the actual items from the SRA Adaptability Test were employed. The same basic format was enlisted—relations and comparisons were explained, debated, analyzed, and integrated. Through lengthy Socratic discussion, Hardy taught his student to examine a question for the exact relation being presented, to carefully discriminate differences among the possible answer choices, and to choose the answer that most nearly matched or fit the requirements of the question. In a sense this was teaching test-taking ability. But it was also teaching intelligence, since the capacity to analyze problems in this way is exactly what intelligence is.

Following 6 weeks of this training, the student scored 14 correct out of the 35 items on the SRA Adaptability Test (Form A), which is about the average score and qualified him for employment. He had originally answered only 2 items correctly. On an alternate form of the test (Form B) the student scored 13, showing that the increase did not stem from previous exposure to the specific test items.

Hardy has not pursued this research, but has become involved in a somewhat different problem. For the past 5 years he has prepared test announcements for police officers taking examinations for job promotion. For example, in a recent announcement that he sent to all officers taking the examination for junior investigator (comparable to first-level detective), he outlined the topics that would be tested by the exam —topics such as the Laws of Arrest and the City Penal Code. In this program, Hardy is not trying to teach basic cognitive abilities; currently employed police officers have already demonstrated adequate comprehension and verbal reasoning ability in qualifying for their jobs. Instead, the announcements are designed to eliminate subtle cultural differences in opportunity to acquire the background knowledge on which passing the promotion exams depends, by making the information openly available to everyone. The program has been a success. Since its initiation, racial differences in promotion exam scores have been completely eliminated. This system of preparation, which Hardy is using in Tulsa, is an example of the type of second-phase program that might follow cognitive therapy in bringing about racial equality in opportunity and employment at all vocational and professional levels.

ARTHUR WHIMBEY, INSTITUTE FOR HUMAN LEARNING, BERKELEY

In a study I reported in the *Journal of Educational Psychology,* college students were taught to solve two-premise deductive reasoning problems. Training was done in groups of five students. During the first session, a Venn diagram method for solving the problems was demonstrated. In later sessions, booklets with problems of increasing difficulty were used. The students all worked the same problem, and then, after sufficient time, one student was randomly selected to explain his solution to the other class members. Subsequently, errors and difficulties were discussed by the class and the instructor. Using this procedure, all the students who initially had difficulty with these problems showed marked improvement as measured by a pretest-posttest comparison.

This study indicated that the ability to solve a certain type of reasoning problem could be improved by training. The question remained whether the broader capacity to deal with all varieties of reasoning tasks—the capacity called general intelligence—could also be improved.

With support from the National Institute of Mental Health, I undertook a study of the thinking processes of students with low scores on academic aptitude tests. The comprehension and reasoning difficulties that I found to be characteristic of such students are illustrated and discussed at length in Chapters IV and V. In essence, I gradually arrived at the same conclusion reached by other experimenters such as Bereiter and Engelmann and Bloom and Broder. Low-aptitude students have not learned how to carefully observe and sequentially combine information in forming relations.

I then began a pilot experiment to train academic intelligence. A student (I shall call him Bob) was selected who had previously taken both the Law School Admission Test (LSAT) and the Graduate Record Exam (GRE). In fact, he had taken the LSAT twice. The first time he scored 385—a low score ranking him at the 10th percentile of the examinees. Subsequently he spent $75 for an LSAT cram course (which met as a 45-student class over a 2-week period) and then retook the LSAT, scoring 372.

His scores at this time on the GRE were likewise low—Verbal Section 380, Math Section 370, for a total GRE score of 750.

The Educational Testing Service, which administers both the GRE and the LSAT, warns that cram courses are relatively ineffective. For example, the booklet sent to students registering for the GRE contains the following statement:

> The Aptitude Test is designed to measure the verbal and quantitative reasoning powers you have developed in the course of your education and general experience. Special study for the verbal sections of the test is not likely to be effective and is not recommended. However, if you have not used mathematics for some time, review of basic algebra and geometry would probably be worthwhile.

Reading comprehension questions (illustrated on page 83) form a major part of both the LSAT and the Verbal Section of the GRE. Bob's low test scores indicated that he had difficulty comprehending and integrating advanced reading material. Therefore, a large portion of the training centered on improving this capacity. Actually, the ability to integrate, analyze, and comprehend verbal ideas, whether they are presented orally or in written form, is a primary facet of academic intelligence, as has been shown by the work of Bereiter and Engelmann, Heber, and others. Thus, training Bob's comprehension ability was also improving his overall academic intelligence.

The procedure used to train comprehension changed somewhat over the course of the program. At the beginning a method of error correction was employed. Bob read a passage *silently* and answered the subsequent questions. Then we picked out his errors and discussed them. This method was reasonably effective. Troublesome questions were reread and reexamined for precise meaning, and Bob's attention was directed to points he had missed. The flaw I found in error correction, however, was that difficult sections might be misinterpreted during the silent reading and be correctly understood later only in a piecemeal fashion, disrupting the overall meaning of the passage. To rectify this, a new procedure was developed.

Bob read a passage *aloud,* and after each sentence or two he interpreted the meaning before continuing. He was required to explain fully what the sentences meant, thinking aloud as he worked through the ideas. Whenever he had difficulty with an idea or a relation, I probed with questions, we discussed the topic, and he tried to reason out the interpretation through a series of deductive steps. Bob was encouraged to interpret each sentence in the context of the entire article and to combine and contrast ideas to attain full understanding.

This method of reading and thinking aloud resembles in many ways the remedial procedure developed by Bloom and Broder. Furthermore, discussing ideas on a one-to-one tutorial basis is the same format used by Blank and Solomon with preschoolers.

Bob's training was not exclusively in reading comprehension. For example, we used verbal analogy problems of the following type:

Hour is to Minute as Foot is to______.

A. Hand B. Yard C. Inch D. Length E. Distance

Here, too, we employed the method of reading and thinking aloud. Bob read the item and was required to explain the relation between *hour* and *minute.* He then discussed how each of the answer alternatives fit, or did not fit, the relation. In this way he learned to analyze problems involving analogy-type reasoning.

To cite one more example, graph-interpretation exercises of the type illustrated in Figure 4 (Chapter V) were employed in a similar manner. Bob read aloud the titles, axis labels, footnotes, quantities, etc. He explained the information being presented and the relations between the several graphs. Then he read a question aloud, explained what it meant, and indicated how he would try to answer it. When he met with difficulty, we discussed the material and I suggested avenues of attack to break the problem into steps and clarify it.

We began the training program—2 hours a day, 4 days a week—in March. Bob took the LSAT at the end of April and scored 432, a gain of some 50 points over his previous scores. We continued training, and in June his GRE total score rose to 820. Shortly thereafter, circumstances forced us to discontinue the training. But this also provided an opportunity to test how really effective the program was—whether we had merely increased test scores or truly augmented thinking capacity.

In September Bob registered for a college algebra class along with other courses. Prior to this, he had always had great difficulty with mathematics: In high school and college he avoided math courses whenever he could, and when a detour was unfeasible his grades were poor. He was unsure of himself this time. However, he found that the training had not only improved his reading of textbooks, but also increased his grasp of class lectures. In essence, lectures are orally presented text and require basically the same activities of comprehension and integration that are used in reading. Bob's scores on class exams went from B+s to As, with a final grade of A for the semester.

Following the class, in December, Bob again took the GRE. His scores were: Verbal Section 460, Math Section 430, for a GRE total of 890—a gain of 140 points over his original score.

Bob is now continuing his education. The gains he made did not come about through a quick-and-easy crash program. Instead, gradually, through intensive training over several months, Bob *began to learn* how to analyze scholastic reasoning problems and how to comprehend difficult text. Now that the proper start has been made, continued practice in academic study may develop these skills further. In retrospect, however, I believe Bob's gains would have been larger and faster had we incorporated the Bloom and Broder procedure into the training. For example, rather than discussing a verbal analogy problem with Bob only after he had attempted to solve it, I believe a more effective method would have been for him to read the written protocol of a model's thinking processes on such a problem. In this way, he would have had a clearer picture of precisely what thorough reasoning and problem analysis consists of. Research on the training of adult intelligence has been more sparse than research with children. Future studies should compare the effectiveness of different training procedures.

This study with Bob, taken alone, would be no more than a suggestive pilot experiment, since only one trainee was involved. However, in combination with the other studies reviewed here—in both its theoretical and methodological agreement—it serves as a further replication of the same general approach to the problem of training thinking capacity.

In considering these small experiments, we may note that Bloom and Broder, as well as Harry Harlow and Herbert Simon (whose works are cited in Chapter V), have called upon psychologists to perform more experiments in which fewer subjects are used for longer periods of time, in order to gather data about long-term learning processes. Certainly using a small number of subjects entails methodological pitfalls. But using many subjects for extended periods tends to be excessively costly, in terms of both money and experimenter time. The apparent remedy is to conduct small pilot studies and then, eventually, extensive experiments that follow up promising leads.

GENERAL CHARACTERISTICS OF COGNITIVE THERAPY

Collectively, the intellect-training studies present a common pattern. Intelligence is taken to be, in large part at least, a habitual approach to problem solving—a learned mental skill. Training this skill is accomplished through demonstration and guided practice. Bereiter (1969) has summarized the contrast between conventional education and cognitive therapy:

> Here is one possibility: thinking, as even the behaviorists are coming to admit, must surely consist of very long strings of actions or responses, most of which are never directly subjected to corrective feedback. Thus learning to think, to the extent that it occurs, must occur under less than propitious circumstances. This would constitute a situation in which inherited differences in functioning of an otherwise trivial nature could have profound effects. Slight differences in immediate memory, alertness, etc., could spell the difference between learning and not learning some of the cognitive behaviors involved in thinking, or between learning them early and learning them late. Yet with a little help they might be learned—help of a kind that is not regularly provided by the feedback conditions of either normal or school life. Educational programs that produce substantial IQ gains may have inadvertently managed to teach such behaviors.

Taking the inadvertence out of training intelligence has entailed two research problems.

The first problem is to define the mental activities that actually constitute intelligence and that, therefore, must be taught. Several experimental views of these thinking behaviors have been summarized, and in Chapter V this topic is discussed in greater detail.

The second problem is to develop techniques that can be used to demonstrate the appropriate mental activities and that can monitor their exercise and growth. It is a well-documented fact of learning psychology that in order for a skill to improve there must be adequate feedback; this feedback has also been referred to, by various psychologists, as *immediate knowledge of results* and *reinforcement of appropriate responses.* Training intelligence presents a special problem because the constituent mental activities are generally carried out covertly —inside the person's head. In order to train intelligence, it is necessary to bring these mental activities to the surface. The methods used to accomplish this include unison response, model's introspective protocol, thinking aloud during practice, and one-to-one Socratic dialogue. Furthermore, individual or small group instruction seems to be a requirement—at least until some other feedback technologies are developed. All these procedures externalize the thinking activities of problem solving so that they can be demonstrated and practiced in full view. It is a point of interest that these methods resemble—and replicate in the classroom—the type of parent-child verbal dialogue in problem solving that researchers believe constitutes the academic advantage middle-class children have over lower-class children.

Externalization of the student's thinking, by requiring continuous response, is a primary tool of cognitive therapy. In this respect cognitive therapy parallels developments in Soviet psychology (Razran, 1961), where covert thinking activities and unconscious emotional reactions are made observable through a combination of classical conditioning and introspection.

Cognitive therapy is a new development in education. In evaluating their own study, Bloom and Broder made the following comment:

> At the onset any new therapy must be considered worthy of further attention if it yields some positive effects and there is

> no evidence of harmful effects. As skilled operators and appropriate subjects are involved, one can demand more and more rigid tests of the remedial techniques.

The impetus for additional research on training intelligence is growing. As it becomes clearer that intelligence is a teachable skill, the need for improved methods of training that skill should become clear to all.

IV. ADVANCED READING COMPREHENSION: A PRIMARY EXPRESSION OF INTELLIGENCE

Intelligence is manifested in many forms. It is used in a wide variety of problem-solving and information-processing tasks. There is, however, one expression of intelligence that occupies a central position in scholastic pursuits—reading comprehension ability.

Although the close connection between reading ability and intelligence has often gone unrecognized by nonspecialists, educational researchers and psychometrists have pointed it out repeatedly. As early as 1917, in a paper entitled "Reading as Reasoning: A Study of Mistakes in Paragraph Reading," E. L. Thorndike analyzed the mental processes involved in reading and compared them to the processes involved in solving a math problem. More recently, Jack Holmes statistically analyzed a battery of reading tests and concluded that reading is a "verbal-processing skill of symbolic reasoning." Edward Fry, in his book *Reading Instruction for Classroom and Clinic,* advised teachers that "intelligence is undoubtedly the chief factor in reading comprehension." And in the *Twentieth Yearbook of the National Reading Conference,* Roger Farr pointed out that from the very first reading test—the Kansas Silent Reading Test, 1916—through current instruments such as the California Achievement Test, questions appearing in tests of reading comprehension ability are almost indistinguishable from questions appearing in standard verbal intelligence tests. For example, the test item called Following Directions (see Appendix 1) was included in both the Kansas Silent Reading Test and the Army Alpha, the first group intelligence test.

In the past few years, IQ testing in the schools has come into disfavor and has decreased. In its place there is now a heightened interest in the administration of reading tests. Educators are finding, however, that the test score distributions obtained with reading tests are almost identical to those obtained with IQ tests: Social class differences persist, and there is the same distressingly high incidence of poor scores. Nothing seems to have changed but the test label. This is readily understood when we recognize that reading comprehension ability is basically one facet of overall academic intelligence. Students with IQs of 85 to 95, within the statistically normal range but on the low side, are generally unable to comprehend and integrate advanced high school and college reading materials. Such students are in need of specific training that teaches them *how* to comprehend and reason with verbal and symbolic sequences of ideas. Prominent reading specialists, such as Miles Tinker, have made this point and have emphasized that the *thinking* side of reading must be taught. With such training, we may expect both overall academic aptitude and comprehension scores to increase. The one positive effect brought about by the change from IQ tests to reading tests is that the task of teaching thinking has now become more tangible and immediate to educators in all specialities and at all levels.

Since the capacity to read with full understanding is the key to all higher learning, the teaching of reading has been isolated as one of the primary objectives of elementary education. Current teaching methods are, however, often ineffective. An article in *Newsweek* (December 11, 1972) posed the following question:

> Is a public school system guilty of fraud if it awards a high-school diploma to a student who can read at only a fifth-grade

level? A San Francisco mother thinks so, and, as a result, her 18-year-old son is suing the city's school district for $1 million.

The mother, whose son filed suit under the pseudonym "Peter W. Doe," claims that her boy has a normal IQ and regularly attended classes; when she became worried about his special reading difficulties, she was told that he was making adequate progress. But when Peter graduated from Galileo High School earlier this year, the suit complains, his reading problem left him "unqualified for any employment other than the most demeaning, unskilled, low-paid manual labor" (his current job consists of moving equipment for a rock-music band). In essence, the suit charges the school district with negligence, misrepresentation and breach of statutory duty.

Whether the California courts will hold a school system legally responsible for graduating a near-illiterate is highly questionable. But this novel law suit—of a type that some educators have been expecting for years—could unleash similar assaults from disgruntled parents across the nation. Many parents, notably blacks and Mexican-Americans, have long complained that teachers shunt their children through the system without properly educating them. But there has never been a definitive measure of a school's legal responsibility for producing graduates who cannot read.

Difficulties: There are many of those. A recent survey for the U.S. Office of Education found that 21 million Americans over the age of 16 lack "the basic reading skills to deal with even the most simple experiences of modern life," such as reading the help wanted ads. What's more, nearly half of all high-school students with reading difficulties never receive help in school, and, even among students who go on to junior college, between a third and a half require remedial instruction in reading.*

There are, of course, many students who do make satisfactory progress with the present teaching methods. The fact that some students develop into good readers, while others who receive roughly the same instruction do not, has led at least one prominent educator to conclude that all reading instruction is ineffective and irrelevant. "Stop Trying To Teach Reading—Just Let It Happen, Expert Says" was the headline of an article in the *Los Angeles Times* on February 25, 1973:

> The best way to get children to read well in school is to stop trying to teach them how, one leading authority says.
>
> Dr. Malcolm C. Douglass, professor of education at the Clairmont Graduate School, thinks that reading cannot be taught directly and schools should stop trying to do the impossible.
>
> "The ability to read," Douglass argues, "is not enhanced by teaching about reading."
>
> Reading is something that must be learned indirectly as a personal, private sort of experience, he said.

Douglass fails to see that within a class of pupils there exist great dissimilarities in home background and preparation. Some students will indeed learn to read with only a minimum of instruction in school. Others, however, need direct training.

READING IS COMPOSED OF TWO SEPARATE SKILLS

Linguists and reading specialists, such as Leonard Bloomfield and Jeanne Chall, recognize that, broadly speaking, reading ability is composed of two separate skills. One is the skill of translating written letter combinations into sounds, so that even nonsense syllables like *tal* and *kib* can be read and pronounced—although no comprehension of meaning need be involved. The second skill is the ability to understand the meaning of what is read.

The fact that these two abilities are distinct does not

necessarily mean they should be taught separately. Experts differ on how the teaching of the two abilities should be combined. The interested reader can find a summary of the contrasting views in Jeanne Chall's book, *Learning To Read: The Great Debate.* Edward Fry's textbook for teachers contains chapters on teaching phonics (related to the first skill) as well as chapters on teaching comprehension. However, Fry's program begins by teaching a small basic vocabulary using the *sight method* so that the child is already reading elementary material with comprehension while he learns phonics. Thus, as the child's reading ability matures, familiar words are read quickly as units, without a laborious letter-by-letter analysis. But when new written words are encountered, the child is prepared to pronounce them phonically.

THE FIRST SKILL: DECODING WRITTEN TEXT

The first ability has been variously called *phonic word analysis skill, decoding skill, word attack skill, word recognition skill,* and *alphabetic habit.* This ability—the ability to simply read words—is, in a certain sense, separable from overall intelligence.

English is one of the most difficult languages to learn to read. It contains approximately 44 primary sound elements, or *phonemes.* Yet it has only 26 letters. Furthermore, some of the letters are pronounced in several different ways and even overlap in their pronunciation. For example, *c* in *cent* represents the same phoneme as *s* in *sense,* but *c* in *cat* is the phoneme represented by *k* in *kept.* To take another example, the letters *th* represent different sounds in the words *though* and *thought.* In spite of this confusion, research has shown that with proper instruction using the *phonic-linguistic method,* any healthy pupil (irrespective of his IQ) can learn the basic letter-sound combinations and word analysis skills that are needed to read primary English words. The pupil is taught what he must look for in reading a word. He is taught all the necessary discriminations and responses (centered on the finite set of 44 phonemes). He already knows how to pronounce all the words in his own speaking vocabulary. He is not required to engage in any new problem solving of a difficult type. And thus, with practice and experience, the reading of words becomes a rote, mechanical process. Only a modest degree of intelligence is needed.

Of course, there are children who do not make satisfactory progress with normal classroom instruction in word attack skills. Children suffering from a hearing defect or any type of visual dysfunction (myopia, hyperopia, astigmatism, lack of binocular coordination) may require special attention.

There are also children who, either because of their home backgrounds or for other unknown reasons, are not prepared to carefully discriminate printed letters on a page or to attend to the lessons presented to the class by the teacher. Some children, for example, must be taught the perceptual skill needed to discriminate similar-appearing letters like *b, d,* and *p.* The preschool programs described in Chapter III have shown great success in teaching reading readiness to such children—preparing them for normal classroom instruction in reading. Furthermore, remedial reading teachers are highly effective in teaching word attack skills to youngsters who have reached the third or fourth grade without having acquired the alphabetic habit. Several days after the Douglass "Stop Trying To Teach Reading" article appeared in the *Los Angeles Times,* the *Times* printed vehement letters from reading teachers who were outraged by Douglass's remarks. They maintained that "any reading specialist worth his salt" obtains 2 months of reading progress for every month of tutoring. They argued that better funding for more extensive remedial programs is needed—not a flight from the problem, as suggested by Douglass.

Until the mid-1960s, effective methods for teaching word attack skills were not widely understood, and since change comes slowly, there are even today children who pass through the primary grades without mastering the mechanics of decoding written text. On the basis of an extensive review of the experimental literature, Jeanne Chall concluded that when the phonic-linguistic approach to teaching reading becomes part of the standard curriculum at all schools (and when it is completely incorporated into the remedial programs used with special problem students), then all healthy children will be able to learn the code and read basic English.

It is still true, however, that children with low IQs have more difficulty than those with high IQs in learning the skill of connecting written symbols with sounds. One approach to this problem—exemplified by the programs of Bereiter and Engelmann and of Heber—is to raise the children's IQs through appropriate training. In fact, such programs have generally included both IQ training and reading readiness training, and under these conditions all healthy children make good progress.

When special IQ and reading readiness training is not offered—as is the case in most schools—children with low IQs sometimes take a year or two longer to master the skill of simply reading words. Furthermore, Chall noted that children with high IQs manage to learn no matter which teaching method is employed. But for children with low IQs, the phonic-linguistic approach is important. If the phonic-linguistic method is used, virtually all children eventually learn to read simple text. Within the normal range of test scores (extending as low as IQ 80), low IQ will not prevent a youngster from learning to translate written text to sounds—it will merely delay his progress. In this sense we can say that the first component of reading—decoding skill—is separable from intelligence.

THE SECOND SKILL: COMPREHENSION

The second skill—understanding connected text—is the phase of reading that is inseparable from intelligence. Easy reading—composed of simple and familiar ideas—requires only a minimum of intelligence. But as the text becomes involved, as facts are compared and contrasted in the course of an extended discussion, as complex relations are described, as ideas are presented that demand active reflection and thought—as problem solving of any type enters the picture—then progressively higher degrees of intelligence are needed for full comprehension.

This is the aspect of reading that educational researchers since Thorndike have pointed to in noting the close relation between reading and problem solving. Ruth Strickland has observed that when linguists speak of "teaching reading" they are referring to the teaching of the first skill—translating written symbols into sounds. To the linguist, teaching the second skill of reading is "teaching thinking." According to Strickland:

> In the eyes of the linguist, a child can read when he can recognize symbol-sound correspondence to the point that he can respond to the marks with appropriate speech. Obviously, the task of teaching does not end here. The rest of what educators call teaching reading the linguist calls teaching *thinking* in response to what is read from the page.

There is much to be said for this distinction. In this view, the burden of teaching comprehension does not and cannot fall solely on the reading specialist. It is the task of all educators.

A large percentage of the high school and college students with "reading difficulties" have, in fact, comprehension problems. Reading specialists who recognize this advise that there is little point in drilling such students in phonics and word attack skills. Such students are usually able to read aloud sample passages from reading achievement tests, thereby showing that they have acquired the skill of alphabetic decoding. But they are unable to answer correctly the comprehension questions that follow the reading passages. And they meet with similar hardship in trying to understand their textbook assignments.

Furthermore, the plight of such poor comprehenders is not confined to reading. It is broader and extends to all areas of academic intelligence. For example, the Stanford-Binet Intelligence Test includes a subtest called Repeating Thought of Passage. The examiner reads a passage aloud, and the examinee is required to demonstrate his full understanding of the material by summarizing the relations and ideas that were presented (he need not repeat the exact wording). Although no reading is required of the examinee, performance on this subtest correlates very highly with scores on standard reading achievement exams—indicating that the same capacity for verbal comprehension is being tapped whether the material is presented orally or in written form. Thus the student who is a poor reader also has difficulty comprehending and benefiting from classroom lectures. Walter Loban wrote:

> Schools are beginning to be aware that research shows a powerful linkage between oral language and writing or reading—one much greater than has previously been realized. This will ultimately bring about reforms in language arts curriculums.

COMPREHENSION: AN ATTENTIONAL SKILL

Some of your own experiences can provide a framework for viewing the roots of poor comprehension. Recall an occasion on which you were required to read while you were fatigued or unmotivated, so that your attention waned—perhaps you were half-heartedly trying to get through a textbook assignment. Quite likely, when you reached the end of the material, you found that your grasp of the more difficult points was vague and unclear. Maybe you realized even in the midst of the reading that you were not giving the material the full attention it demanded; but you continued, wanting to be finished but lacking the incentive to concentrate and work at detailed analysis.

You may question how this experience relates to the problem of the inept reader, since your problem was simply lack of application to the task at hand. Consider a second example.

Have you ever read unfamiliar material *aloud,* before a group of people, with your thoughts distracted by anxiety about your presentation or disturbed by some difficulties of unusual pronunciation? On finishing, you may have been left with only a superficial acquaintance with the material: Complex arguments and deeper knowledge were lost along the way. In this case, lack of application was not at fault. Indeed, the peculiarity of this example is that every single word was read aloud, demonstrating a definite quality of concentration. And yet, because attention to the train of meaning was disrupted, comprehension was diminished.

A somewhat related experience can be had by turning on a radio news report to high volume and then reading aloud. Though the words are read, background noise jams attention, and understanding is lost.

I noted a similar lack of comprehension when I proofread a manuscript for a colleague. At his request, I concentrated solely and intently on the correct spelling of individual words —to the exclusion of conceptual interpretation. I had virtually to reread the whole paper to find out what he had said. This phenomenon was described by Miles Tinker as follows:

> The successful proofreader must constantly ward off the tendency to become absorbed in the meaning of the text. Crosland . . . discovered that proofreaders miss many errors when they attend too much to meaning. And untrained proofreaders have much greater difficulty in resisting this tendency. The professional proofreader, if he is to be an expert, must avoid attending to meaning so that he may be set specifically to discover typographical errors.

All these examples depict the importance of intentionally *attending to meaning* in achieving comprehension. And this pinpoints the characteristic that distinguishes capable readers from incapable readers. The primary cause of poor comprehension is that the unskilled reader has not learned to attend carefully to meaning.

Good readers occasionally read without attending to meaning, but generally they are aware of their loss. By contrast, poor readers have virtually no perspective about what thorough understanding really is. Poor comprehension is a facet of low intelligence; and low intelligence is a habitual thinking pattern characterized by little attention to the analysis and discernment of exact relations. To gain improvement, the poor reader must be taught the features of good comprehension. He must have the minute details of complete understanding demonstrated and illustrated to him.

This view of poor comprehension is in keeping with Bereiter and Engelmann's observation that culturally disadvantaged preschoolers are not concerned about or cognizant of the gaps in their knowledge. The cognitive habit of pursuing complete understanding is foreign to them until it is taught. Similarly, Bloom and Broder have reported that low-aptitude college students are insensitive to the fact that they have read superficially and that they inadequately understood the instructions in problem solving. Furthermore, they are satisfied with a guessed answer to a question. Such is their habitual orientation in thinking.

When the inferior reader tries to read, what he really does is skim the material in a manner that resembles inattentive perusal. However, this is his habitual pattern, rather than the result of a temporary loss of motivation. Such habitual skimming leaves him unable to follow involved arguments that require detailed thought, and so he comes away from a reading selection with only its more evident facts and concrete descriptions. The poor reader has not learned to analyze and construct meaning. Instead, when he answers reading comprehension questions, he draws from his superficial understanding of the material and combines this with his prior opinions on the topic. This deficient processing can be illustrated by a sample of reading comprehension errors made by students whom I have tested.

COMPREHENSION TEST ERRORS

A common, though not invariable, symptom of poor comprehension is reading too quickly. Bloom and Broder noted how hastily low-aptitude students read directions to problems. This symptom is also illustrated by an incident that occurred while I was testing a student on a type of examination that is included in the Law School Admission Test (LSAT).* Five articles were to be read in 15 minutes. An additional 15 minutes was then allotted for answering a series of questions from memory—without referring back to the articles.

The student and I each had a copy of the exam. I took the test along with the student in order to understand better his thinking processes and errors. The stopwatch set, we began reading.

Completing the first of the five articles—about 650 words long—I looked up at the stopwatch and saw that 2.25 minutes had passed. I then glanced at the student and found that he was already in the middle of the third article. It struck me that he could not possibly be forming a clear, detailed picture of the material. We continued. After 6 minutes the student had finished all five articles and was back at the beginning for a second pass. In fact he eventually went through a third time, more quickly still. Then he began answering the questions. A portion of the first article is reproduced below:

*In the actual LSAT, three articles, somewhat more difficult than the three illustrated here, must be read in 15 minutes, after which questions must be answered from memory. In addition, the LSAT includes the usual type of comprehension test in which the examinee may refer back to the articles while answering questions.

With increasing prosperity, West European youth is having a fling that is creating distinctive consumer and cultural patterns.

The result has been the increasing emergence in Europe of that phenomenon well known in America as the "youth market." This is a market in which enterprising businesses cater to the demands of teenagers and older youths in all their Beatlemania and pop-art forms.

In the United States, the market is wide ranging and well established, almost an industry, which with this country's emphasis on "youthfulness," even extends beyond teenager groups.

In Western Europe, the youth market may appropriately be said to be in its infancy. In some countries such as Britain, West Germany and France, it is more advanced than in others. Some manifestations of the market, chiefly sociological, have been recorded, but it is only just beginning to be the subject of organized consumer research and promotion.

Characteristics of the evolving European youth market indicate dissimilarities as well as similarities to the American youth market.

The similarities:

The market's basis is essentially the same—more spending power and freedom to use it in the hands of teenagers and older youth. Young consumers also make up an increasingly high proportion of the population.

As in the United States, youthful tastes in Europe extend over a similar range of products—record players, transistor radios, leather jackets and "wayout," extravagantly styled clothing, cosmetics and soft drinks. Generally it now is difficult to tell in which direction trans-Atlantic teenage influences are flowing.

Also, a pattern of conformity dominates European youth as in this country, though in Britain the object is to wear clothes that "make the wearer stand out," but also make him "in," such as tight trousers and precisely tailored jackets.*

*Turner (see Bibliography).

The entire article was about twice this length and continued to compare American and European patterns. Questions of the following type were asked:

The "youth market" in our country

A. refers to others besides teenagers
B. refers to adults who act like teenagers
C. is confined to "Beatle-worshippers" and "pop-art" devotees
D. has come into being within the last few years
E. refers to anyone who feels young

The passage states or implies that the youth market is more established in

A. France than it is in West Germany
B. Italy than it is in France
C. Belgium than it is in Sweden
D. England than it is in our country
E. our country than it is in England

Although the article is far from technical, the student chose alternative C for the first question, because, as he later explained, he recalled that pop-art and the Beatles had been mentioned. Evidently, only these labels had caught his attention in the second paragraph, where the youth market is defined. Paragraphs two and three describe the age groups encompassed by the youth market. But in both cases the information is embedded in sentences that also present other ideas. A good reader carefully separates the ideas and thus forms a clear image of whom the youth market refers to. The poor reader, however, lacks the habit of analysis that underlies the proper processing of information.

For the second question the student chose alternative A because he "knew France was a hipper country than Germany." The various comparisons between countries made in the article had been missed entirely.

The articles included in this test were of only intermediate difficulty, since the test was designed to measure recall as well as comprehension. When the student was later permitted to refer back to the selections (rather than answer from memory), he pinpointed the necessary information—although sometimes with difficulty—and answered almost all the questions correctly.

However, the poor reader's unanalytical skimming does irreparable damage to his understanding of complex material where interpretation in context and gradual construction of meaning are indispensable.

Cursory skimming is the habitual approach of poor readers, not just a pattern confined to time-limit tests. With untimed tests, poor readers whom I have tested often perused a reading selection very quickly—sometimes finishing before good readers had even reached the halfway mark. But the inadequacy of their attention became evident in even the most basic type of question answering. They frequently had no idea whatsoever about where in a given passage the necessary information could be located, and had to begin rereading almost from scratch. Good readers, by contrast, invariably had some knowledge of the selection's structural layout: They knew roughly what points had been made in which paragraphs and could locate pertinent facts quickly.

The skimming of deficient readers can hardly be called reading. The main gist of an article may be missed entirely, and specific facts are misinterpreted because they are read completely out of context. The importance of careful reading is illustrated in the following exercise:

> Some scraps of evidence bear out those who hold a very high opinion of the average level of culture among the Athenians of the great age. The funeral speech of Pericles is the most famous indication from Athenian literature that its level was indeed high. Pericles was, however, a politician, and he may have been flattering his audience. We know that thousands of Athenians

sat hour after hour in the theater listening to the plays of the great Greek dramatists. The plays, especially the tragedies, are at a very high intellectual level throughout. There are no letdowns, no concessions to the lowbrows or to the demands of "realism," such as the scene of the gravediggers in *Hamlet.* The music and dancing woven into these plays were almost certainly at an equally high level. Our opera—not Italian opera, not even Wagner, but the restrained, difficult opera of the 18th century—is probably the best modern parallel. The comparison is no doubt dangerous, but can you imagine almost the entire population of an American city (in suitable installments, of course) sitting through performances of Mozart's *Don Giovanni* or Gluck's *Orpheus?* Perhaps the Athenian masses went to these plays because of a lack of other amusements. They could at least understand something of what went on, since the subjects were part of their folklore. For the American people, the subjects of grand opera are not part of their folklore.

The author's attitude toward Greek plays is one of

1. qualified approval
2. grudging admiration
3. studied indifference
4. partial hostility
5. great respect*

A student read this article without a time limit and was permitted to refer back to it freely as he answered the questions. For the question above, he chose alternative 1.

I asked him to explain his choice and he answered, "The article said that Athenians may have attended the plays because they had nothing better to do, not because they were good." I asked what else the article said, and he replied, "Pericles may have merely been flattering the Athenians, their culture may not have been that outstanding."

Such misunderstanding and confusion of ideas are com-

*Gruber (see Bibliography).

mon among poor readers. In this case the student had not formed a distinct picture of the author's opinion of Greek plays as contrasted with the author's opinion of average Greek culture.

The ideas and comparisons presented in this article are more involved than those of the passage about the youth market. Greater care and active construction over a broader extent of text are required to establish a clear picture of the discriminations and relations. Even after the student was told that he had chosen the wrong answer, he was unable to piece the author's ideas together and select the correct alternative. The poor reader does not know how to read properly because he has not learned to think in a pattern of careful analysis—a pattern that is the very heart of intelligence.

Lack of careful analysis is illustrated also in the following example:

> Sometimes the meaning of the glowing water is ominous. Off the Pacific coast of North America, it may mean that the sea is filled with the dinoflagellate *Gonyaulax,* a minute plant that contains a poison of strange and terrible virulence. About four days after Gonyaulax comes to dominate the coastal plankton, some of the fishes and shellfish in the vicinity become toxic. This is because, in their normal feeding, they have strained the poisonous plankton out of the water. Mussels accumulate the Gonyaulax toxins in their livers, and the toxins react on the human nervous system with an effect similar to that of strychnine. Because of these facts, it is generally understood along the Pacific coast that it is unwise to eat shellfish taken from the coasts exposed to the open sea where Gonyaulax may be abundant, in summer or early fall. For generations before the white men came, the Indians knew this.
>
> The title below that best expresses the main idea of this passage is:
>
> 1. minute plants
> 2. the feeding habits of *Gonyaulax*

3. what the Indians knew
4. danger from the sea
5. the human nervous system*

The student chose alternative 2. I asked him what he meant by the term *feeding habits*—for example, the feeding habits of his dog. He thought for a few seconds and replied, "How the dog eats." Then I asked whether the article was about the feeding habits of *Gonyaulax.* He checked to find *Gonyaulax,* read a little further, and then said, "No, it's about how *Gonyaulax* are eaten by fish and fish can then poison people." With further discussion it became clear that initially he had not only skimmed and misinterpreted answer 2, but had also skimmed the article itself. All he had gathered from it was that it had something to do with feeding and a "fish" called *Gonyaulax.* Thus, alternative 2—the feeding habits of *Gonyaulax*—was an attractive guess.

This example illustrates a pattern that continually recurs in the testing of poor readers on material of intermediate difficulty. The student misinterprets some portion of the material, is asked to reread it, does so slowly and often painfully, and then frequently emerges with a better understanding. The youth market exercise illustrated the same pattern, and similar observations were reported by Bloom and Broder (Chapter III). The regularity with which low-aptitude students are able eventually to obtain a better grasp of the material supports the conclusion that habitual, inadequate processing, rather than neurologically based conceptual incapacity, is the cause of poor comprehension. By contrast, in the more involved article on Greek culture the entire interpretation was set awry by the habitual skimming of ideas. The poor reader's approach left him unable to organize and discriminate the multiple themes even when he was asked to reconsider the material.

*Gruber (see Bibliography).

This is illustrated again in the following example:

> If a serious literary critic were to write a favorable, full-length review of *How Could I Tell Mother She Frightened My Boy Friends Away,* Grace Plumbuster's new story, his startled readers would assume either that he had gone mad or that Grace Plumbuster was his editor's wife.*

This was the first sentence of a reading comprehension article, and I had to stop for a moment and reread a portion of it in order to understand its meaning completely. Not so the low-aptitude student I was testing. He was halfway down the page by the time I had the details of the first sentence sorted out. I asked him if he had understood the sentence, and he answered, "No, not really." So I suggested he give it another try. He examined it for a while, but then said he could not get it. So we probed at it together, first discussing whether the pronoun *his* (third word from the end) referred to the startled reader, to the author Plumbuster, or to the critic, and we eventually got the entire picture clarified.

Why was the student unable to comprehend this sentence? Not because the concepts are too abstract or theoretical, but because the sentence requires multiple steps and sequential interpretations. First one point has to be clarified and then the reader can proceed to the next step. The good reader does this in such a habitual manner that he is hardly aware of these mental activities. Only when he meets with an especially intricate or confusing series of ideas does his sequential sorting become "intentional" and conscious. To the poor reader, however, the pattern of gradual, sequential construction of exact meaning is totally foreign. One-shot thinking (Bereiter and Engelmann's term) is the basis on which the poor reader makes interpretations and draws conclusions.

The inferior reader is unpracticed and incapable of seeing

*Gruber (see Bibliography).

relations embodied in difficult text. The form of this inability bears some similarity to the ineptitude of a novice biology student looking through a microscope for the first time. Both stem from a lack of cultivated acquaintance with relevant responses and discriminations. Just as the novice biology student has not learned how to direct his attention in resolving the conundrum he finds on a laboratory slide, the inferior reader has not learned how to attend to meaning—how to make a detailed analysis of verbal ideas. Both microscopy and comprehension are attentional skills, and both are trainable. However, the admonition to "pay attention" is not very helpful in training either skill. And in the case of reading, the advice to "read slower" or to "read more carefully" is also, by itself, insufficient. The student needs guidance of the type provided by Bloom and Broder in teaching academic thinking. He must be taught *how* to attend to meaning; he needs to be informed about exactly what the constituent mental activities are.

THE MENTAL BEHAVIORS OF GOOD READING

The primary and distinctive mark of a good reader is that he continuously seeks to construct an accurate picture of a writer's intent. When he is reading seriously, he never ceases attempting to form a precise mental replica of the relations that are being presented in verbal symbols by the text.

Full comprehension begins with attention to every single word, every phrase, and every sentence of the material. Words that are familiar are immediately understood. Less familiar words and phrases are translated into comfortable synonyms or perhaps into instantaneous and fleeting visual images. Tinker has said:

> To recognize a word means to identify it as a word previously known, i.e., the visual form of the printed symbol leads to correct revival of the sound of the word, with association between the sound and the sound's meaning and the visual form.

> Immediate or relatively rapid recognition occurs only with words that are well known through frequent encounters in previous reading. But other words which a reader has met but which are less familiar are recognized less promptly, usually after a slight delay.*
>
> To illustrate the process, consider the following sentence:
>
> Perturbation, bordering on riot, occurred in the House Saturday after President Ferdinand declared martial law and ordered that all utilities be taken over by the military.

A collage of associations, gathered from the reports of several good readers who read this sentence, took the following form:

> "Perturbation" was not immediately clear until "bordering on riot" was read; then the synonym "disturbance" suggested itself. Which "House" was not evident until expanded to "the House of Representatives." "Saturday" was felt as a movement to several days earlier in the week. "President Ferdinand" was a foreign leader, perhaps Spanish or South American. "Utilities" flashed as the gas company. And "martial law" became clear only when "taken over by the military" created an image of soldiers.

No single person had all these associations, but this represents the type of active processing that occurs when good readers read.†

A good reader proceeds smoothly and quickly as long as his understanding of the material is complete. But as soon as he senses that he has missed an idea, that the track has been lost, he brings smooth progress to a grinding halt. Advancing more slowly, he seeks clarification in the subsequent material,

*Tinker (see Bibliography).

†A more extensive discussion of visual, kinesthetic, and other such associations to verbal communications can be found in Aleksandr Sokolov's book, *Inner Speech and Thought.*

examining it for the light it can throw on the earlier trouble spot. If still dissatisfied with his grasp, he returns to the point where the difficulty began and rereads the section more carefully. He probes and analyzes phrases and sentences for their exact meaning; he tries to visualize abstruse descriptions; and through a series of approximations, deductions, and corrections he translates scientific and technical terms into concrete examples. The mental activities involved in reading a legal contract or a physics textbook illustrate these operations well. Detecting the exaggeration in the following sentence is not difficult, but it does demonstrate the process of translating verbal symbols into other forms.

> The hurricane raged with such fury that palm trees leaned 98 degrees from the vertical.

In checking their understanding of this sentence, many good readers, in effect, visualize some image of the vertical—perhaps picturing actual palm trees—and then, by making an arc of more than 90 degrees, come to recognize the full power of the storm.

Bloom and Broder have reported that a major difficulty of low-aptitude students is their failure to convert abstract or unfamiliar terms and phrases into concrete and intelligible ideas. The steps of careful comparison and deduction through which this is accomplished are what low-aptitude students must be taught.

VOCAL ACTIVITIES DURING READING

Recent studies have disclosed that good readers, while reading difficult material, often pronounce each word subvocally so that the words are distinctly heard in the mind's ear. This contradicts popular educational advice (especially as expounded by speed reading courses), which insists that readers should avoid all traces of subvocal speech. Small activities of the vocal apparatus are considered to be a poor reading habit, and lip movement is especially taboo.

While I was a college student—and at the time unacquainted with the scientific research on reading comprehension—I was on several occasions filled with concern about my reading habits. The "antivocalization" writers, in their books on reading improvement, demanded that I stop covertly pronouncing words as I read them. I was to make no lip, tongue, or throat movements, or even "hear" the words mentally. But to me subvocal speech was the most comfortable manner of careful reading, and since altering the habit seemed so unpleasant (it was so mentally taxing to read very carefully without subvocalizing), I never made more than a token effort in that direction. Yet in the back of my mind I always felt an uneasiness about not trying harder to stop all vocal activities and mentally to silence the words as I read. Recent discussions with students in my classes indicate that many of them have been equally confused by the antivocalization advice.

The question of whether vocal involvement is a bad reading habit—one that is detrimental to good comprehension and characteristic only of poor readers—has special relevance to the discussion of IQ-training methods. Reading aloud while attempting reasoning problems and comprehension exercises is an integral part of several of the cognitive therapy formats discussed in Chapter III. Requiring the trainee to read and think aloud is the tool whereby the direction of the trainee's mental activities is monitored and guided. If vocalizing were indeed a poor reading habit, then the use of reading aloud as a method for training academic intelligence might be questionable.

A number of recent studies (such as those by Ronald Carver, Ake Edfeldt, Curtis Hardyck and Lewis Petrinovich, F. J. McGuigan) have investigated the issue using various experimental techniques, including sensitive electronic recording devices. These studies indicated that good readers as well as poor readers make small lip and tongue movements while they read. Two other points came to light. First, as material becomes more difficult, covert speech increases with both good and poor readers, indicating that subvocalization is somewhat like low gear of an automobile and is especially useful for understanding complicated text. Second, subvocal speech is definitely not the *cause* of poor reading, and it is not detrimental to comprehension. The data indicated that, if anything, it is a crutch on which poor readers lean for help.

What is the origin, then, of the notion that vocal involvement is a poor reading habit? Basically the idea arose from the misinterpretation of observations of students with reading difficulties.

Some children with reading problems, as well as near-illiterate adults, have not mastered the first of the two skills of reading discussed earlier: They have not mastered decoding skill. They have trouble reading individual words and struggle to pronounce each one. Their vocalizing is obvious, and from it, early experimenters drew the conclusion that vocalizing is the *cause* of their poor reading ability. In many respects, their difficulty is similar to that of an educated American who has learned to speak German (perhaps while visiting the country) but who has never read the language. In trying to read a postcard written in German, he painfully deciphers and pronounces each word aloud so that he can hear it and thus recognize it. Obviously in these cases vocalizing is not the cause of poor reading, but a symptom of the difficulty. Thus there is no point in discouraging vocalization as such. Instead, the individual must gradually be taught to read words fluently through instruction in word attack skills.

Vocalization occurs also when word reading is adequate, but comprehension skill is lacking. For material at any specified reading difficulty level used in a laboratory reading test, poor readers may vocalize more frequently and overtly than good readers because the material is harder for them and they fall back on first gear more often. But here again, vocalizing is not the cause of their problem, but only a symptom.

Yet another complication shrouds the issue of vocalization: the question of what criterion is used to define *good reading.* Do we mean *speed* or *comprehension?* Some educators contend that reading can proceed most speedily if all elements of vocal involvement are minimized. And so, if the criterion of good reading is reading speed, then vocalizing may be a bad reading habit. But vocalizing does not hinder comprehension.

Actually, there is still some question about whether vocalizing really reduces reading speed. E. C. Poulton has found that it is possible to read *aloud* at up to 425 words a minute. Furthermore, numerous researchers, such as John Carroll of the Educational Testing Service, have concluded that reading of any type, silent or otherwise, cannot proceed much faster than this without some loss of comprehension. For example, Robert Dixon reported that the average reading rate of a sample of 48 University of Michigan professors (presumably good readers) was 303 words a minute. Similarly, the average reading rate of Harvard freshmen was found by Paul Kolers to be around 300 words a minute. It thus appears that vocalizing would not seriously reduce the reading speed of most good readers, since their normal reading rate is slower than their top vocalizing speed.

One situation is perhaps an exception. With very easy or redundant material, a person need not read every word, but can skim and skip without much loss of comprehension. In such a case pronouncing each word would retard progress. It appears that vocalizing reduces only skimming speed, but not true reading speed.

Good readers not only "hear" the words as they read and make small lip and tongue movements, but they may go so far as to whisper a difficult phrase or sentence in grasping its meaning. When this is done with an attitude of seeking understanding, the kinesthetic involvement seems to intensify concentration and fix ideas more strongly in mind. More than likely you have done it yourself—you have read a sentence that was unclear, gone back with your brow knitted in concentration, and whispered the words just below the level of hearing so that the sentence attained a deep grip on your attention.

Copying a sentence verbatim, while trying to understand its meaning, is another method of using physical involvement to focus concentration. Mathematicians, whose daily fare is an extremely concise, difficult language, often start by recopying a portion of a statement or an equation as they search its meaning. While the symbols are slowly copied and thought through, every element comes into detailed view, and new perspectives have a ready chance to develop.

Reading aloud (especially when someone is listening) with careful attention to enunciation and presentation may interfere with comprehension because it draws attention away from the train of meaning. But private speech is different. Vocalizing while reading is a form of talking to oneself, and many people find talking to themselves a good way to think —an effective method for clarifying ideas. They do not usually speak aloud, but their lips often move a little. In the *Seventeenth Yearbook of the National Reading Conference,* David Wark reported that good readers often talk to themselves at the ends of sentences and that this appears to aid their comprehension. Talking to oneself in a quiet, rationally organized manner is not a sign of mental derangement, although it is sometimes facetiously depicted as such. Instead, it is a useful tool of cognition and problem solving. Similarly, subvocalizing and even mouthing words are legitimate ways of reading. This does not mean that a person must vocalize if he does not need to or if it is not natural to him; it does mean that vocalizing should be used freely whenever it is helpful. Recent data collected by the Soviet researcher, Sokolov, have a strong bearing on this point.

In a series of experiments, Sokolov tested subjects on arithmetic and figural reasoning problems while at the same time recording the electrical activity of their speech musculature. As the problems became progressively more difficult, the amplitude of the laryngeal electromyogram systematically increased. This was true until the problems became so difficult that they were unsolvable. Then motor speech impulses ceased. Motor speech impulses were also reduced when mere repetition of a response was required rather than new problem solving. From these data, Sokolov concluded that vocal activity is not confined solely to the reading of intricate text or to the solution of purely verbal problems; vocal responses occur while grappling with a variety of exacting mental tasks. This study ties reading comprehension together with other expressions of intelligence. In the next chapter I shall argue that all comprehension, analysis, and problem solving are composed of small gradual constructions rather than instantaneous, full-blown abstractions. The vocalization measured by Sokolov is one concrete manifestation of such active mental processing.

Cognitive therapy requires the student to read aloud. This may entail a certain awkwardness at first, but the student readily adapts to the procedure. For one thing, a smooth, polished oral presentation is not required. Furthermore, the student is permitted (even encouraged) to reread material when necessary for complete understanding. Thus, an occasional difficulty of pronunciation presents no special hardship. The student's attention is primarily focused on comprehension and analysis. Bloom and Broder's report (together with discussions I have had with Jim Hardy of Tulsa and my own research experience) shows that students quickly develop the ability to read and think aloud without serious interference with their problem-solving activities.

READING SPEED

While discussing vocalization, I referred to studies that bear on another misconception about reading, namely, that good readers are continuously swift, that slowness is a sure sign of reading difficulty. This idea stems from a misunderstanding of *why* poor readers read slowly.

One reason poor readers read slowly is failure to master the skill of decoding. Children with word-reading difficulties stumble, struggle to pronounce words, and sometimes substitute their own words for the words in the text. For example, in the sentence "The kitten went into the store" a 7-year-old who has difficulty reading the word *store* may hesitate, make several attempts, and eventually read, "The kitten went into the storm." Such children read both slowly and inaccurately.

Poor readers whose word-reading ability is satisfactory, but who habitually skim and whose comprehension is therefore deficient, are likewise slow and hesitant when they are required to read accurately in a test situation. Their lack of practice in reading for meaning and their shallow store of verbal knowledge and vocabulary leave them ill prepared for answering questions. They read and reread the material trying to select correct answers, but are unable effectively to grasp the ideas.

The apparent paradox is that good readers are also slow when they read difficult text; they take time to attain complete understanding and to ponder ideas. For instance, earlier I cited a study in which the average reading rate of University of Michigan professors was found to be about 300 words per minute. This is a rate that many reading programs regard as slow and in need of improvement. But apparently the Michigan scholars adopt this rate in bringing associations and images to mind that fully clarify the written ideas, and in integrating relations that, in some cases, may be separated by several sentences or even paragraphs of text. In a somewhat compulsive manner they habitually sacrifice speed for carefulness, accuracy, and reflection.

Alfred Binet's definition of intelligence has relevance to the discussion of reading processes. Binet wrote:

> That which is called intelligence, in the strict sense of the word, consists of two principal things: first, perceiving the exterior

> world, and second, reconsidering these perceptions as memories, altering them and pondering them.*

Good comprehenders have learned to approach difficult reading material in the careful analytical way that Binet describes as the essence of intelligence. The text (the "exterior world") is perceived carefully, and then the perceptions are reconsidered and reflected on in constructing a complete interpretation.

These activities of reconsidering, altering, and pondering are not instantaneous—they take time. Paul Fitts and Michael Posner, viewing the reader as an information-processing system, have described the restriction such activities place on reading speed:

> In coming to understand [a book or story], the subject must impose upon the words he hears or sees transformations which include selection, combination, and classification. To the extent that such transformations are involved, they should be manifested, as in other tasks, in the reduction of the rate at which the information can be assimilated. That is, the requirement to transform information will require a portion of the central processing mechanisms which will then be unavailable for dealing with new information from the story.

This view is supported by the following observation made by Bloom and Broder in their study on training academic ability:

> Several of the students in the problem-solving program were attending a program in remedial reading. This program is designed to increase the speed of reading and to raise the level of comprehension in reading. For a few of these students, the remedial-reading instructor reported that after the problem-solving training their speed of reading had decreased, although their level of comprehension had increased.

*From a translation by Pollack and Brenner (see Bibliography).

All this indicates that slow reading may be a sign of reading difficulty, either because of ineptitude in word reading or because of lack of skill in comprehending connected text. But slow reading is not in and of itself a symptom of poor reading ability: Good comprehension of difficult text also proceeds slowly.

Instructing a poor comprehender to try to read faster, which is often done, is in no case a useful remedial measure. Instead the student must be properly taught the reading skills in which he is weak. Tinker, after years of research and teaching experience, has offered the following advice:

> In general . . . throughout elementary school, the emphasis should be placed upon development of comprehension, word meanings, and concepts. If this program is properly carried out, there will be little need for specific training in speed of comprehension for most pupils. Any class-wide program for "whipping up" the speed of comprehension represents misplaced emphasis. When the program of teaching is adequate, speed will tend to take care of itself. "When material is within the child's capacity to understand, the more clearly he comprehends it the faster will his rate of progress tend to be" (Tinker & McCullough).

SPEED READING COURSES

In sharp contrast to the type of reading program suggested by Tinker, speed reading courses make speed the primary focus of reading instruction. Speed reading courses and their advertisement campaigns have influenced both popular notions about reading ability and reading programs within formal education. Therefore, their procedures and claims deserve some attention.

Speed reading instructs the student to skim down the center of the page, rather than reading from left to right, and to aim for a rate of 1000 or more words per minute. In this way, no sentence is completely skipped, but each is merely touched on. Theoretically, speed reading (when pursued by a person who is already a good reader) differs from poor reading in that it does emphasize attention to comprehension and active construction of meaning; there is a mental set to try to understand. But the question is, How much can possibly be gathered and understood while the reader's eyes are racing directly down the center of a page?

It should be obvious from the previous discussion of reading as thinking and analysis of relations, that speed reading cannot possibly impart comprehension of new and complex ideas, but can only provide a superficial acquaintance with topics. For many purposes, and much reading material, this may be all that is required. But more cannot be expected.

The claim is sometimes made that speed reading will triple your comprehension. But the reading tests used to substantiate this claim statistically are really tests of acquaintance, not comprehension. The only fair statement is: Speed reading will triple the rate at which you can be exposed to material.

A typical speed reading exercise might start with an article detailing the mishaps, tactics, and decisions involved in Washington's crossing of the Delaware. "Comprehension" is then measured by questions of the following type:

> The best title for this article is:
>
> 1. The Construction of the Lincoln Tunnel
> 2. Crossing the Delaware During the American Revolution
> 3. Factors Leading to the American Revolution
> 4. George Washington's Childhood Education

"Comprehension" is measured by the number of easy questions answered after a fixed period of reading time. With easy questions, the more ground covered, the more questions answered. Ronald Carver's book, *Sense and Nonsense in Speed Reading,* examines more extensively the violations of sound psychometric measurement committed by speed reading and exposes other fallacious claims.

If speed reading really improved comprehension, it would be a boon to students taking the SAT, GRE, and LSAT. These tests depend heavily on the ability to comprehend difficult text. But none of the speed reading schools to date claims to improve scores on such tests. They would immediately be faced with a charge of false advertising.

Perhaps the most telling lie of speed reading is its insistence that the reader never "regress"—that he never reread words or sentences. Speed reading training emphasizes that readers sometimes feel uncertain about their understanding of a sentence, but that they must learn to ignore this feeling and keep going, because comprehension will not suffer. Now this is obviously nonsense. It is often necessary to reread some section of material in order to grasp its full meaning. The statement that comprehension will not suffer is founded on a statistical lie. Comprehension, measured in absolute terms, does suffer—even on the simple comprehension tests used by speed reading courses.

A speed reading class I attended had as its stated objective: "increasing reading rate while not dropping below 70 percent comprehension." One student, for example, started at 400 words a minute at 90 percent comprehension and "progressed" to 1300 words a minute at 70 percent comprehension. The instructor of the course argued that 70 percent of 1300 (which equals 910) was more than 90 percent of 400 (equals 360) so that comprehension per time unit was increased. The weakness in this statistical juggling is evident. In an absolute sense, 70 percent is lower comprehension than 90 percent; 70 percent comprehension means that 30 percent of the material is missed. I personally do not want a surgeon who understands 70 percent of his medical text, or an automobile mechanic with only 70 percent comprehension of auto repair. For that matter, when I read a joke in the course of a novel, I don't care to come away with only 70 percent of the punch line.

In a study recently conducted at the University of Redlands, Richard Graf demonstrated that speed readers lose comprehension. College students were pretested with reading materials that varied in difficulty from easy to hard. The test was composed of selections from *Doctor Zhivago, Playboy, Redbook,* and a psychophysics textbook. The students then spent several weeks in a speed reading course, after which their reading ability was again tested. For both the easy and the difficult material, reading speed increased, but comprehension decreased. In terms of overall averages, speed rose by 221 percent while comprehension dropped by 39 percent.

The failure of some educators to distinguish reading power from reading speed—the failure to understand the processes underlying good comprehension—has led to the inappropriate use of speed reading courses with pupils who actually are badly in need of basic training in comprehension skills. A study reported by Myron H. Dembo and Donald A. Wilson in the May 1973 issue of *Phi Delta Kappan* (see Appendix 3) illustrates this point.

READING COMPREHENSION AND INTELLIGENCE

Oral comprehension, reading comprehension, and skillful reasoning and thinking appear to be closely related activities. In fact, there is a developmental connection between the abilities. The 1964 Research Conference on Education and Cultural Deprivation observed that children from disadvantaged homes have had insufficient practice in attending to extended speech sequences and that this leads to ineptitude in all extended reasoning. In other words, typically the growth of thinking skill begins with the development of listening comprehension ability at home and continues with the development of reading comprehension and advanced reasoning ability in school. The preschool programs of Bereiter and Engelmann and of Heber basically replicate this sequence:

They focus on the child's language comprehension and verbalized thinking and thereby establish a basis for overall academic readiness.

There is at present no reason to assume that this developmental sequence is fixed. With older students it may be expedient to teach thinking skill in the context of training the ability to comprehend and analyze written material. This is suggested in part by the studies of Bloom and Broder, Hardy, and Whimbey. Such a relation between training reading comprehension ability and intelligence has important implications for public education. The teaching of overall academic thinking ability by the elementary and secondary schools could be effectively organized around reading comprehension training. This would parallel the language/thinking emphasis of the IQ-stimulating preschool programs. Teaching the mental construction processes that constitute careful reading for meaning might go a long way toward eliminating social class differences in academic intelligence.

V. INTELLIGENCE: A LEARNED SKILL

The error many psychologists and educators make in trying to understand intelligence is to view it as a unitary dimension, such as the physical dimension height, and then to attempt a one-sentence definition. As a result, the only definition of intelligence on which all psychologists agree is that "intelligence is what intelligence tests measure." Psychologists recognize the limitations of this definition—that it is circular and does not actually describe intelligence. In addition, they know that intelligence is much more than merely a person's ability to score well on IQ tests. (For example, studies show a high correlation between IQ test scores and academic attainment.) Nevertheless, it has been impossible to formulate a more satisfactory definition of intelligence while approaching it as a unitary dimension.

The intelligence-training studies reviewed in Chapter III indicate that intelligence is a complex mental skill. As such, it can no more be defined as a unidimensional characteristic than golf skill or swimming skill can be defined in that way. Instead, an adequate definition lists the major activities that are carried out to achieve some specified end. A complete definition of swimming skill, for example, describes the various limb and body movements used in propelling the body through water. Before presenting an analogous description of intelligence, two common misconceptions of intelligence deserve mention.

INTELLIGENCE IS NOT SYNONYMOUS WITH LEARNING CAPACITY

Intelligence tests have always found their greatest validity in predicting school grades, and because of this some early researchers concluded that IQ tests measure overall learning and memory capacity. (For example, Edward Thorndike theorized that persons with high IQs have more neural connections available to learn and remember facts and to form relations among complex ideas.)

If IQ and learning capacity were synonymous, persons who score high on IQ tests should be able to learn lists of randomly chosen numbers more quickly than those who score low on IQ tests. This is easy to investigate experimentally and, in fact, has been subjected to numerous studies. Following the administration of IQ tests, the subjects were given various types of materials to learn—lists of numbers, or letters, or nonsense syllables. The lists were presented in stimulus-response pairs or in randomly ordered series, and retention was tested over short periods of time or over longer intervals. All possible variations were tried; yet study after study failed to establish any relation between primary learning capacity and intelligence. Instead of a close correspondence between the abilities, some persons with high IQs did quite poorly at learning lists of syllables or numbers; and some extraordinary performances in elementary learning were displayed by persons of modest IQs. The evidence was unequivocal: Intelligence was not simply learning capacity.

Herbert Woodrow performed the definitive study in this area 30 years ago, and anyone interested in examining the topic in more detail might well begin with his article entitled "Interrelationships of Measures of Learning," published in the *Journal of Psychology,* vol. 10, 1940.

Woodrow's study, along with many other experiments in the area, indicated why measures of learning and memory do not correlate with IQ: Such measures do not even correlate highly with each other. Consider, for example, the learning measure called Memory Span, in which the subject is presented with a series of digits, such as 8–5–6–3–7–9, and asked to recall the series immediately. Healthy adults differ in Memory Span ability—some can recall only five digits whereas others recall as many as nine. But the interesting thing is that Memory Span ability does not correlate highly with other learning and memory measures (French et al., 1962). In fact, among healthy adults, each type of memory ability appears to be specific unto itself; no overall memory ability has been isolated (Jensen, 1962). Instead, there is memory for serial lists, memory for paired associates, symbolic memory, semantic memory, figural memory, long-term memory, short-term memory, etc., and each of these categories breaks down even further. The reason for this specificity is apparently that each type of memory requires a different pattern of organization and background experience. In view of this specificity, it is not surprising that among healthy adults memory and learning measures do not correlate with IQ.

David Wechsler, originator of the widely used Wechsler intelligence scales, pointed out the lack of relation that exists between memory ability and intelligence, and discussed the implications this has for the practical problem of measuring adult intelligence:

> Memory span, whether for digits forwards or backwards, generally correlates very poorly with all other tests of intelligence. . . . For a long time we considered the desirability of eliminating the test from our battery altogether, but finally decided to retain it . . . [because] while memory span for digits backwards and forwards is on the whole a poor measure of intelligence, it is nevertheless an extremely good one at the lower levels. . . .
>
> Rote memory more than any other capacity seems to be one of those abilities of which a certain absolute minimum is required, but excesses of which seemingly contribute relatively

> little to the capacities of the individual as a whole. The Memory Span for Digits test has the great merit of quickly indicating whether an individual has the relative minimum.

All healthy adults have this minimum. Wechsler concluded that the Memory Span test finds its primary use in diagnosing extreme feeblemindedness, organic disease, and other abnormal conditions.

Herbert Simon reported a study that adds greatly to our understanding of memory ability and its relation to other mental capacities. Simon's study was not directly concerned with IQ, but it illustrates the general finding that superior problem-solving ability does not presuppose any unusual primary memory capacity. It thus substantiates Wechsler's point that while a certain minimum memory ability is necessary, beyond the normal minimum, memory contributes little to a person's thinking capacity.

Simon (with an associate, William Chase)* wondered whether chess masters were possessed of an appreciably better visual memory than other humans. A chessboard, with the pieces prearranged, was presented for just 5 seconds of study to a chess master, a player of intermediate strength, and a novice. The pieces were placed in a pattern that corresponded to the middle of an actual chess game. Then the pieces were removed, and the subjects of this experiment were asked to recall the positions from memory. The novice recalled only 4 positions, the intermediate player recalled 8 positions, and the master recalled an average of 16 positions correctly.

In the second phase of the experiment, Simon and Chase made one small procedural change. The same subjects were used, the same chessboard, the same 5-second viewing interval, but this time the pieces were positioned *randomly*—the arrangement was not one that could have occurred in an actual

*See Simon and Chase (1973) for a review of the variations of this experiment that have been performed by other experimenters.

chess game. When the recall scores were tallied, a most essential fact of memory was demonstrated: The master now recalled no more than the weaker players—all three players averaged less than 4 positions correct.

In summarizing this study, Simon noted that chess masters are able to code "real game" information into familiar chess patterns. He estimated that after studying chess for several hours each day, over 10 years or more, a master can recognize between 10,000 and 100,000 patterns—patterns involving both stationary positions and active strategies of attack. However, without the use of such a coding pattern, the memory of a chess master is, like that of everyone else, quite limited.

Simon and Chase's experiment confirms the conclusion of earlier research: Individual differences in pure memory do not correlate with differences in problem-solving ability. More to the point, many other experiments have shown in an analogous fashion that neither limited memory nor restricted learning capacity is related to, or is at the basis of, low IQs in healthy adults.

INTELLIGENCE AND ABSTRACT THINKING ABILITY

Although no definition of intelligence is professionally recognized by all psychologists, many psychologists (and laymen) implicitly think of intelligence as the ability to do abstract thinking. For example, Lewis Terman, who translated the original Binet test for American use, took this as his definition of intelligence.

In contrast to the learning ability theory of intelligence, the abstraction ability theory has not generated any research. This is because it does not provide a really clear definition of intelligence—one that can be pinned down and experimentally verified. It does contain a kernel of truth, but it depicts intelligence in a way that prevents continued progress in understanding mental development. Furthermore, it often carries with it the implication that abstraction ability is dependent upon genetically determined neurological superiority. Keith Hayes (1962) made this point with the following comments:

> Such a function [abstraction ability] has commonly been conceived of as a genetically determined brain power, which the individual has more or less of, and which he can use in all appropriate situations.

Hayes's 1962 *Psychological Reports* article included a thorough, critical review of the term abstraction ability. The interested reader will find the article most informative. Donald Hebb (1945), Seymour Sarason (1959), and other writers have also indicated the faults of abstraction ability theories. Several examples are illustrative.

The formal definition—intelligence is the ability to do abstract thinking—encounters trouble as soon as the word *abstract* is sought in the dictionary. It means "thought of, or conceived of, apart from specific cases." By this definition, every adult who is free of neural pathology is capable of abstract thinking.

In Chapter I, I quoted passages in which Kurt Goldstein argued that patients with certain brain lesions are not able to think abstractly. But, by contrast, all healthy adults are conversant with common abstractions such as *squareness, circularity,* and *whiteness.* Even broad abstractions such as *"catness,"* encompassing the characteristics that distinguish all members of the feline family—domestic cats, leopards, tigers, and wildcats—are familiar to most adults. Obviously, then, the mere ability to think abstractly is not a useful dimension for distinguishing high intelligence.

Apparently what Terman and other psychologists who use this definition mean is that superior intelligence is characterized by the ability to cogitate difficult, or high-order, abstractions. But this definition encounters another complication. How do you define the difficulty of an abstraction? Herein lies the weakness of the abstraction ability theory of intelligence. The statement "Intelligence is the ability to think with high-order abstractions" is theoretically empty because there is no psychologically meaningful scale on which the abstractness of concepts can be gauged.*

As an illustration, consider the ideas *jump, add, comprehend,* and *cheat.* How would you measure precisely which of these ideas is more abstract? Is the idea of *adding* more abstract than the idea of *jumping?* Be careful not to be confused by the fact that one of the activities (adding) is largely mental and the other activity (jumping) is largely physical. We are discussing the concept or the idea of adding and the idea of jumping—both of which are mental; we are not discussing the activities themselves.

Intuitively and loosely speaking, *comprehending* seems a highly abstract concept. But semanticists and metaphysicians would be hard-pressed to specify how the concept *comprehending a textbook* is more abstract than the concept *adding columns of numbers.* A person might argue that thinking about *comprehending* can involve *more* thinking (*more* mental activity) than thinking about *adding.* Indeed, a little reflection shows that when we characterize a concept as more abstract, we mean roughly that it requires *more* sequential and comparative thought. And, as later discussion will show, the notion of *more* thinking comes close to Binet's original definition of intelligence. This notion, however, leads to a completely different perspective on intelligence than that implied by the abstraction ability theory.

Semantics textbooks sometimes cite cases in which concepts can be ordered by abstractness or generality, but these are special cases that have scant relevance for intelligence

*It is noteworthy that Piaget used the terms *concrete operations* (ages 8 to 12) and *formal operations* (beyond age 12), rather than *concrete operations* and *abstract operations.* Thereby he avoided the ambiguity of the word *abstract.* Furthermore, all adults are capable of formal operations (Hunt, 1961).

measurement. Concepts can be ordered by abstractness when they can be placed into a hierarchy of the type illustrated in Figure 2. The higher the position in the chart, the more abstract the concept.

In this arrangement, high-order concepts include low-order concepts—*fruit* includes orange and apple. Moreover, high-order concepts include elements that differ more widely from each other than do the elements of low-order concepts. That is, the elements included in the concept *fruit* (Jonathan, tangerine) differ more from each other than do the elements subsumed by the concept *orange* (navel, tangerine).

But most ideas and words cannot be compared hierarchically: There is no way to relate *apple* and *jump,* or *jump* and *comprehend,* in this manner. And so, for the majority of concepts, there is no objective basis on which to scale abstractness.

Undoubtedly all classification systems, all generalizations, all summaries are abstractions. But the abstraction is the final product, not the process, of thinking. It is also true that persons differ in their ability to construct and properly use abstractions. This is because they differ in their tendency to bring all thinking into comparative and relational focus, not because of cerebral limitations or impoverished neural complexity.

VOCABULARY AND INTELLIGENCE

Vocabulary tests are a principal tool of psychometric measurement. They are, undoubtedly, among the easiest tests to construct, and they appear in almost all the major published scales of mental capacity. While vocabulary may not be the purest measure of intellectual strength (Charles Spearman, for example, preferred nonverbal reasoning questions of the type illustrated on page 118), vocabulary is a good indicator. The question is, Why does vocabulary reflect intelligence?

If you have had occasion to read test manuals, you have probably come across a test description that explains that the items (the words) in the test are arranged according to

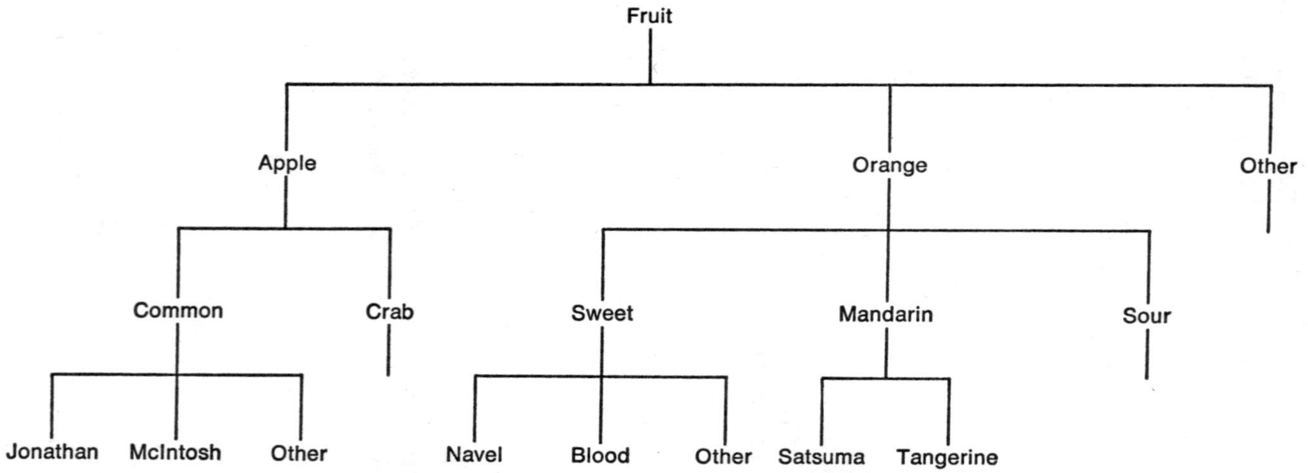

Figure 2. Hierarchy of Abstractness for the Concept *Fruit*

progressively greater verbal abstractness. Moreover, the explanation continues, persons of low intelligence are not capable of making high-level abstractions—ergo, they do not understand many of the words, and they score poorly. But now comes the crucial question: What does the manual mean by verbal abstractness?

This point is usually glossed over quickly with a "self-evident" example. *Automobile,* the explanation says, represents a low level of abstractness. *Justice* and *democracy* represent the highest level. But do you find *democracy* on the test? No. How about *justice?* No again. Why? Because, in fact, both these words are part of the speaking vocabulary of every American adult—even those with IQs of only 80 or 85. Instead, if you examine a number of vocabulary tests you will find them stocked with esoteric expressions for rather simple ideas—words like *amulet, prowess, tepid, prologue,* and *epilogue.*

I am not criticizing vocabulary tests. My point is that abstraction ability does not truly explain their validity. Why then does vocabulary reflect intelligence? The reason is that vocabulary knowledge is an end product of the processes that underlie what in Chapter IV was called the second skill of reading—the skill of comprehension. In other words, vocabulary knowledge accumulates, and is practiced, in the course of fully comprehending verbal ideas. And as such it is a good indicator of overall intelligence.

To be sure, some concepts do demand more thought—more comparative analysis—for their comprehension, and we sometimes refer to these concepts as more abstract. However, understanding such concepts requires not greater neural endowment expressed as a mythical abstraction ability, but rather a reflective pattern of thinking.

BINET'S DEFINITION OF INTELLIGENCE: MENTAL RECONSTRUCTION

The definition of intelligence as the "ability to do abstract thinking"—with the associated notion that this ability is genetically determined—has proved an empty theoretical model. It has contributed little, if anything, to psychology's understanding of the mental activities that underlie intelligence. Nor has it aided the design of better psychological tests. The progress that has been made in test construction has come about primarily through empirical research and modification, using a statistical technique called item analysis whereby the most efficacious test items are selected and retained in a test for future use.

A more serviceable definition comes from Alfred Binet, the pioneer researcher of intelligence At an early stage in his career, in 1890, Binet wrote:

> That which is called intelligence, in the strict sense of the word, consists of two principal things: first, perceiving the exterior world, and second, reconsidering these perceptions as memories, altering them and pondering them.

Nineteen years later, what was to remain basically Binet's final and subsequently unchanged view of intelligence took the following form:

> In our opinion, intelligence, considered independently of phenomena of sensibility, emotion and will, is above all a faculty of knowing *(connaissance),* which is directed toward the external world, and which labors to reconstruct it as a whole, by means of the small fragments of it which are given to us. What we perceive of it is element *a,* and all the very complicated work of our intelligence consists in uniting with this first element a second element, the element *b.* All knowing *(connaissance)* is thus essentially an addition, a continuation, a synthesis, whether the addition takes place automatically as in external perception . . . or after a conscious search. . . . But note well that in this addition to the element *a,* there is already a host of faculties at work: comprehension, memory, imagination, judgment, and above all, speech. Let us retain only the most essential, and, since all this culminates in the invention of an

> element *b,* let us call the operation an *invention,* which is executed after a *comprehension.* The operation cannot be performed without our knowing what the question is, without our adopting a certain line, from which we do not deviate; thus a direction is necessary. . . . The ideas must be judged as fast as they are produced and rejected if they do not fit the end pursued; there must, thus, be *censorship.* Comprehension, invention, direction, and censorship; intelligence is contained in these four words.

Note the abundant detail of mental operations contained in these definitions compared with the rather nonpsychological statement that intelligence is abstract thinking ability. These are descriptions of the actual dynamics of intelligence, gleaned by the method of comparative introspection—by questioning children about their thoughts during problem solving.

In the course of his research, Binet observed that intelligence is composed of perception and then reflection. The latter process consists of combining elements and actively forming mental reconstructions of the world. Self-censorship plays an important role in this process. At other times Binet used the term *autocriticism* in referring to a person's activities of judging whether an "invention" is complete and correct, or whether more data and more construction are necessary.

Arthur Jensen, in the opening pages of his controversial *Harvard Educational Review* paper, described the mental attributes needed to profit from traditional classroom education:

> . . . the ability voluntarily to focus one's attention where it is called for, the ability to comprehend verbal utterances and to grasp relationships between things and their symbolic representations, the ability to inhibit large-muscle activity and engage in covert "mental" activity, to repeat instruction to oneself, to persist in a task until a self-determined standard is attained.

This description bears a strong similarity to Binet's definition of intelligence. Jensen's "focus one's attention where it is called for" and "persist in a task until a self-determined standard is attained" may be aligned with Binet's "perceiving the exterior world," "direction" and "censorship." And Jensen's "grasp relationships between things and their symbolic representations" is the *end product* of Binet's "reconsidering these perceptions as memories, altering them and pondering them."

The experiments in cognitive therapy are in complete agreement with Binet's definition. Cognitive therapy teaches the student to perceive the external world accurately and to reconsider the perceptions. It teaches the mental pattern of pondering experiences, of sequentially constructing relations.

The observations on poor reading comprehension reported in the previous chapter are also in agreement with Binet's dynamic view of intelligence. Poor comprehenders are habitual skimmers, both of the reading material and of their own stores of knowledge. They have never learned to direct their attention fully and carefully to the relevant external stimuli (the text) or to reflect on and reconsider the material in constructing accurate interpretations.

Hunt (1961) has pointed out that Binet did not regard intelligence as genetically fixed. In fact, Binet urged strongly against the hereditarian view. If his untimely death in 1911 (at age 54) had not brought his process-oriented research to an end, the history of mental testing might have taken a different course. Hunt quoted the following passage from Binet (1909):

> Some recent philosophers appear to have given their moral support to the deplorable verdict that the intelligence of an individual is a fixed quantity. . . . We must protest and act against this brutal pessimism. . . . A child's mind is like a field for which an expert farmer has advised a change in the method of cultivating, with the result that in place of desert land, we now have a harvest. It is in this particular sense, the one which

is significant, that we say that the intelligence of children may be increased.

THE MENTAL ACTIVITIES OF INTELLIGENCE

The intelligence-training studies reviewed in Chapter III have extended Binet's observations by specifying the mental activities characteristic of persons with high IQs and the errors made by persons with low IQs. The following example is drawn from my own research.

Figure III presents a figural reasoning problem. Figural reasoning is considered by many psychometrists as the purest measure of reasoning ability because it minimizes vocabulary knowledge and other obvious products of formal education.

Consider the steps leading to a correct solution of this problem. First the four figures must be accurately compared. Figure II is visually different from figure I: Since discrete lines compose the shading, counting suggests itself as a probe. Indeed, figure II has two fewer vertical lines.

Comparison of figure III with figure II shows horizontal shading to have decreased by one line, with vertical shading unchanged. Figure IV in turn is figure III save two vertical lines.

Gathering these changes into a continuous sequence yields: delete two vertical lines, delete one horizontal line, delete two vertical lines. If now the sequence is viewed as a consistently structured rule, the next change should be: delete one horizontal line—which points to alternative D.

This somewhat difficult figural reasoning problem is a good measure of intelligence. It would, however, never be presented in isolation like this, but would be preceded by easier warm-up problems; otherwise it might be missed even by persons of high IQ. Can its difficulty be accounted for by an abstraction ability concept of intelligence? Not readily. Neither the dimensions of vertical and horizontal, nor the rule (delete two vertical, delete one horizontal, etc.) is very abstract. Then why is the item missed?

INSTRUCTIONS. The first four figures below change in a systematic manner according to some rule. Your task is to discover the rule and choose from among the alternatives the figure which should occur next in the series.

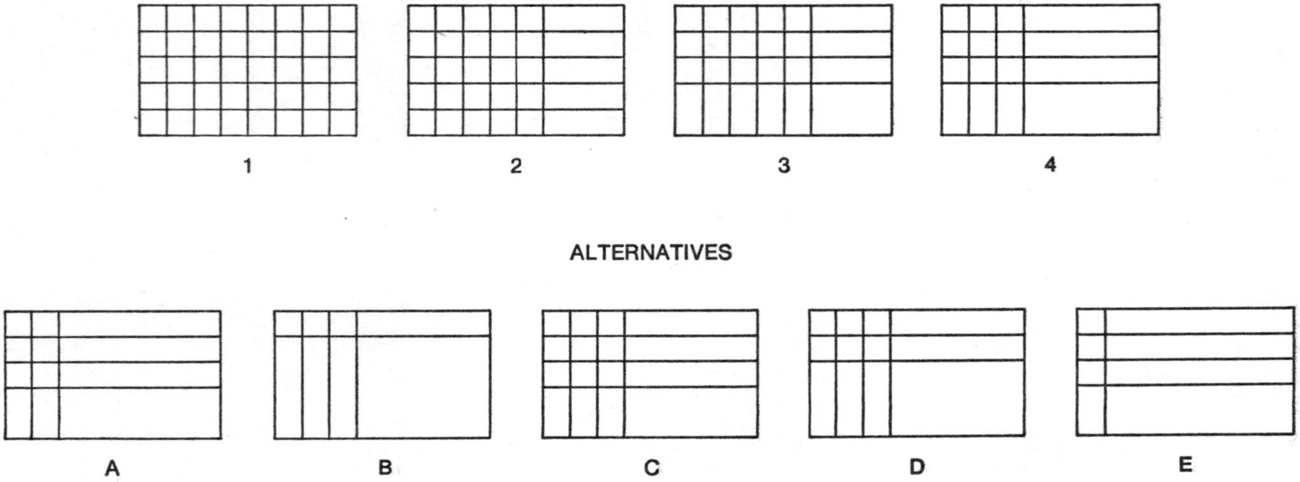

Figure 3. Sample Figural Reasoning Problem

Alternative B was chosen by one person who later reported that he knew that one or two lines were to be deleted, but was not sure which. Another person who missed the item chose alternative A because he was confused about whether to take one line from the horizontal or the vertical. The most perplexing error was the choice of alternative C, which is identical to figure IV and incorporates absolutely no change. Yet the error occurred often and speaks directly to the nature of intelligence.

At first sight, these errors seem to be the result of limited memory capacity: Deficient memory would prevent a person from following all the details of the problem. But research has shown that memory is not a factor in the IQ of healthy adults. Instead, on the basis of the various observations cited in Chapter III, a different picture of intelligence emerges. *Intelligence is paying careful skilled attention to the analysis of relations.*

Though somewhat simplified, this appears to be the sum and substance of intelligence. The simplification resides in the phrase "paying careful skilled attention." Just as a novice biology student must learn *how* to look through a microscope—must develop discrimination in learning *what* to look for by actively separating some elements and combining others—so intelligence consists of knowing how to direct attention in discerning relations.

As noted at the beginning of this chapter, a full definition of any skill consists of a description of major activities carried out in achieving some end. In formulating a definition of intelligence, I compiled a list of the major mental activities that distinguish the problem solving of persons with high and low IQs. I then incorporated this list into the framework of Binet's definition of intelligence. The resulting definition of intelligence is, undoubtedly, only one dimension of a complete theory of thinking; other researchers may analyze intelligence at different levels and arrive at alternative perspectives. However, this definition does summarize the common core of mental activities that the training experiments reviewed in Chapter III seem to have focused on—the mental activities that differentiate the successful processing of persons with high IQs from what Bereiter and Engelmann have called the one-shot thinking of persons with low IQs. This definition, presented below, will, I hope, be useful to other educators developing and employing procedures to train intelligence.

> Intelligence is an attentional/processing skill used in analyzing and mentally reconstructing relations. The distinguishing feature of this skill is breaking complex relations (or problems) into small steps that can be dealt with fully. The major components of the skill are extensive search and careful apprehension of all details relevant to the relation; thorough utilization of all available information including prior knowledge; accurate comparisons; and sequential, step-by-step analysis and construction.

THE SPECTRUM OF HUMAN SKILLS

You may have reservations about accepting the mental behaviors included in my definition as the distinguishing components of intelligence, and your reluctance may stem mainly from the question, "If intelligence is simply a set of skills, why are some people so much more intelligent than others?" Well, why are some adults good swimmers whereas others flounder and sink? Why are there good athletes—gymnasts, football players, expert equestrians—whose swimming might be described as optimistic splashing? The answer involves a multitude of reasons, some environmental (lack of encouragement and opportunity to practice) and others, perhaps, genetic. But an instructional method that regards swimming as a pattern of skills can make almost anyone a competent swimmer. And in a similar way the method of cognitive therapy appears able to teach almost anyone reasoning, comprehension, and other facets of intelligence.

A number of researchers have pointed out the similarities between physical and mental skills. Sir Frederick Bartlett, in his book *Thinking,* wrote:

> It seems reasonable to try to begin by treating thinking provisionally as a complex and high-level kind of skill. Thinking has its acknowledged experts, like every other known form of skill, and in both cases much of the expertness, though never, perhaps, all of it, has to be acquired by well-informed practice. Every kind of bodily skill is based upon evidence picked up directly or indirectly from the environment, and used for the attempted achievement of whatever issue may be required at the time of the performance. Every kind of thinking also claims that it is based upon information or evidence which, again, must be picked up directly or indirectly from the environment and which is used in an attempt to satisfy some requirement of the occasion upon which the thinking takes place.
>
> It would be easy enough to go on pointing out a number of other likenesses, or a similar general character, between bodily skill and thinking.

Fitts and Posner reinforced this point in their book *Human Performance* by demonstrating that symbolic skills (such as reading comprehension ability) and perceptual-motor skills (such as hitting a baseball) are basically subject to the same laws of development and performance. They stated:

> The spectrum of skills is a broad one and includes both the organization of sequences of movements and the organization of sequences of symbolic information.

Moreover, Fitts and Posner introduced their discussion of reading and listening comprehension with the following remarks:

> This chapter will be concerned primarily with an analysis of complex skills involving what may be called higher mental

> functions—for example, thinking and problem solving, which depend at least in part upon language. [Such] skills will be studied through an analysis of their component functions, in much the same way as has been done for perceptual-motor skills.

Bloom and Broder made an important application of the similarity of physical and mental skills in their aptitude-training study. They found that in training college students it is helpful to point out to the trainee the close connection between learning a physical skill such as tennis and learning the thinking patterns of academic reasoning. This description provided the trainee with an understanding and an orientation toward the program.

ATTENTIONAL/PROCESSING SKILLS (LEARNING SETS)

Attentional/processing skills are closely related to the broad psychological phenomena termed *selective attention.* All perception and information processing, all thinking, is dependent on selective attention. Holding a conversation in the midst of a crowded, noisy party demands attending to one set of auditory stimuli while filtering out and ignoring distractions. Listening to a record twice, the first time focusing on the song's words and meaning, and the second time concentrating on the instrumental arrangement—perhaps the variations and flights of the congo drum—also illustrates the human capacity to make a shift in psychological amplification. In a more academic vein, adding a column of numbers requires that attention be turned to the business of addition, rather than to the visual and aesthetic qualities of the printed numerals.

In many cases the ability to direct attention appropriately and to discriminate and process the information that is relevant to some task improves with practice. This acquired proficiency is an attentional/processing skill. The examples of selective attention cited above are subject to such improvement, for instance, when a novice musician learns to separate and distinguish the sounds of different instruments, pitch ranges, rhythm patterns, and chord progressions—when he develops a "musical ear."

The perceptual aspect of driving an automobile furnishes another illustration. A seasoned driver has an easy familiarity with the road because he knows exactly what to look for and what is important. Except for emergencies and traffic snarls, he can travel for hours and unnoticed miles deeply engrossed in conversation with a passenger because his mind is attuned to the numerous decisions of driving and his eye is familiar with the relevant cues. An occasional glance in the rear-view mirror updates his continuous awareness of surrounding vehicles. He has learned to perceive, to sort, to retain for a short interval, to judge, to combine, and to anticipate the conditions of surface transport. Innumerable hours of experience and practice lie behind the attentional/processing skill that separates the competent driver from the fearful, confused driving trainee.

Phonic word analysis is yet another attentional/processing skill. It is a skill that has academic relevance, although it differs from the configuration of skills called intelligence. It is a narrower skill, concerned only with the pronunciation of unfamiliar words, not with the analysis of new relations. Phonic word analysis is explained most readily by contrasting it with the whole-word approach to pronouncing unfamiliar words.

Most modern reading programs teach a small number of basic words by the whole-word or sight method, and then also provide the child with extensive training in phonic word analysis skill. Thus, as the child's reading ability matures, familiar words are recognized quickly as wholes without a tedious letter-by-letter breakdown, whereas unfamiliar written words can be analyzed and sounded out effectively. However, according to Jeanne Chall, for about 50 years whole-word reading dominated American elementary reading education, to the complete exclusion of instruction in phonic analysis. In fact, even today (says Chall) some reading programs still do not give sufficient emphasis to the teaching of word attack skills.

In the old whole-word approach, the child was only taught to view words as essentially integral units. He was given little or no instruction in viewing words as aggregates of constituent syllables and letter combinations. Consider, for example, the word *chocolate*—part of most children's speaking vocabulary. In school, the teacher would simply write *chocolate* on the blackboard and read it aloud; the child learned the visual pattern of the word, which is quite unlike that of other words, and thus came to recognize *chocolate* when he saw it in print. However, the whole-word method never rigorously taught the sounds of individual vowels, consonants, and common English letter combinations like *ch, sh, sch,* and *tia* (as in *initial*). Nor did it emphasize the technique of analyzing new words into distinct letter-sound elements. The result was that many children—and even some adults—frequently mispronounced new written words by confusing them with similar-appearing familiar words, and by adding or deleting letters and syllables. *Aerobics* might be pronounced *aerobatics, magenta* pronounced *magneta, incentive* as *incenative,* and *commutative* as *cumulative.*

In the course of one experiment, I tested a 24-year-old college senior whose comprehension and overall academic intelligence was good, but who had been taught to read exclusively by the whole-word method and who tended to mispronounce unfamiliar written words. I presented the printed word *vociferate* and he pronounced it *vocaferanate*—the first two syllables sounding like *vodka* without a *d.*

I asked him to please try it again.

"Vocfernate."

"Try it once more."

"Vocafernate."

I pointed out that there was no *n.*

"Vocaferate."

This was close. The last two syllables were right, but the first two were still pronounced like *vodka.* I asked for one more go at it. The correction required changing *c* as in *come* to *c* as in *cent;* pronouncing the *i* as in *if;* and making the *o* long. But the student had no experience with phonic analysis, and his mind drew a blank.

With proper instruction, and a fair amount of practice, any healthy student can readily learn phonic pronunciation. New words are then resolved through the fine apperception of distinct syllables and letters. Attention becomes familiar with this type of analysis, and with experience, the sounds taken by sundry letter combinations become ready knowledge.

Intelligence, like phonic pronunciation and driving, is an attentional/processing skill. Parallel to the phonic analysis of words into letter-sound elements, intelligence is the learned facility to work through the details of relation analysis by making a series of observations, informational interpretations, comparisons, and constructions. Among skills, intelligence is unique only in the extent to which its activities are internal and concealed from view.

Talents can be arranged on a scale according to the overtness of component behaviors. The elements of golf—choice of club, bodily stance, movement, swing, follow-through—are in large part observable and are thus readily demonstrated, criticized, and corrected through guidance. Automobile driving is similar in this respect. Long division occupies an intermediate position on the scale because answers to subpart computations are periodically written so that they can be seen and corrected by a teacher. Intelligence, however, is at the furthest extreme of covertness: The entire sequence of comparisons, interpretations, and constructions underlying figural reasoning or reading comprehension is private and hidden. This concealment has not only deterred the education of intelligence, but has totally shrouded its status as a collection of specific and definable behaviors. The problem of covertness is avoided in cognitive therapy by requiring constant responding, verbalizing, and thinking aloud. Intelligence is thus brought to the surface. Its constituent activities become susceptible to what is variously called guidance, feedback, and reinforcement. And its development is put on par with driver education and the teaching of phonics.

HARLOW'S RESEARCH ON LEARNING SETS

The notion of an attentional/processing skill has its roots in the now classic research of Harry Harlow (1949), although Harlow referred to such an aquired skill as a *learning set.* I shall describe Harlow's research in broad outline; the reader may refer to Harlow's original report for the more technical details.

Harlow seated a monkey in a special testing apparatus that contained two cups. One cup had a red cover over it and the other had a green cover; a grape was always to be found under the red cover. On the first trial, the red cover was placed over the left cup, and the monkey found the grape through trial and error. Then a screen was lowered to prevent the monkey from seeing the manipulations, and a grape was placed in the right cup with the red cover over it. Untrained monkeys tend to look for a reward in the position in which it was found last. Thus, when the screen was raised, the monkey sought the grape in the left cup, which in this case had the green cover and was empty. Trial-and-error learning continued—with the red cover being randomly switched from left to right—until gradually, over a number of trials, the monkey learned to pick the red cover directly.

Next, Harlow presented the monkey with another problem—a blue and a yellow cover, the yellow one always signifying the grape. Again the monkey required a number of trials to learn always to pick the yellow cover. The monkey was then presented with another problem of colored covers, and then another one, and then another. Each time he learned to choose the correct color.

However, something changed. With successive problems, the monkey required fewer and fewer trials to master the discrimination. In fact, after approximately 300 different problems, the monkey learned how to solve this type of problem immediately. When presented with a new pair of colors, his choice on the first trial was, of course, a guess. But if by chance he chose the correct color, he stayed with it on successive trials—even though it moved from the left side to the right side randomly. And if by chance he chose incorrectly on the first trial, he immediately shifted to the correct color on the second trial and then stayed with it.

Harlow pointed out that as a result of the training, the monkey's learning ability increased. On the first problem he required a number of trials before he learned to choose the correct color. After training, he required only one trial—the first trial—to learn which color was correct. The monkey had become prepared to learn material of this type; he had learned to pay attention to and utilize the information that was significant in this class of learning situations. The monkey had learned *how to learn,* and Harlow labeled this process the formation of a *learning set.*

Harlow has demonstrated the development of other learning sets. For example, in the reversal experiment, a monkey was first taught that red was correct and green was incorrect. Then Harlow suddenly made green correct. Naturally the monkey made errors, and it took him some time to learn that red was no longer correct. However, when Harlow continued periodically to switch colors in this manner for about 100 problems, the monkey gradually learned to deal with the situation. Then, as soon as Harlow switched colors, the monkey switched his response on the immediately succeeding trial. The monkey had learned to disregard the information from all prior trials and to pay attention only to the most recent outcome.

In discussing intelligence I have used the term *attentional/processing skill*—rather than Harlow's original term *learning set*—because it is more descriptive and presents a fuller picture of the phenomena. Referring to the attribute as a *skill* stresses that it is an acquired behavior (the word *set* does not make this clear). Furthermore, *attentional/processing* points out that skillfully focusing attention and processing relevant information constitute the heart of any learning set.

Regardless of which term is used, an important point to recognize is that acquiring a learning set (or attentional/processing skill) corresponds to *improving learning ability in a specific area.* When Harlow's monkey had acquired the object-color learning set, he was able to learn quickly—in just one trial—how to get a grape immediately. As another example, consider phonic word analysis. Mastering the skill of phonic word analysis has not always been regarded as increasing a type of learning ability, but this is really what occurs. Phonic word analysis skill allows a person to *learn how to pronounce* an unfamiliar written word quickly. Without this skill a person might be required to ask someone else how the unfamiliar word should be pronounced. IQ or intelligence is the skill that assists in the learning (the mental reconstruction) of relations that are not perceived immediately but require active analysis. Thus, while IQ tests do not measure overall innate learning potential, they do reflect a broad and useful acquired learning ability.

THE SKILLED OPERATIONS OF INTELLIGENCE

In defining intelligence I listed four primary mental operations that are carried out sequentially in problem solving. These were illustrated in Figure 3. The problem involved careful apprehension of figural details, drawing on prior knowledge (such as counting), accurate comparisons between figures, and construction of an encompassing rule. Another illustration of the skills of intelligence is the popular verbal analogy test item. An example is presented below:

Elbow is to Shoulder as Knee is to______.
A. Foot B. Ankle C. Hip D. Wrist

The details of this problem are words. Words are symbols for objects and ideas, so their meanings must be called to mind from prior knowledge. Persons of low intelligence translate *elbow, shoulder, knee,* etc. But then, being unskilled in analysis, they pick an answer based on an insufficiently detailed consideration of the relationship "is to–as–is to." *Foot* might be chosen as an answer, on the "reasoning" that *elbow* and *shoulder* are parts of the arm, while *knee* and *foot* belong to the leg. Or the alternative *ankle* might be selected, because it is a joint, as are *elbow, shoulder,* and *knee.* High intelligence goes further.

The anatomical relation between *elbow* and *shoulder* is visualized, or examined on the body, and then compared successively with the relations formed by *knee* and each of the alternatives. Moreover, several of the latter relations may be compared with each other—for example, *knee-ankle* contrasted with *knee-hip*—to bring their singularities into focus. With careful persistence it becomes readily apparent that *hip* is the correct answer—that *shoulder* and *hip* are proximal joints, located where the respective limbs attach to the body, and thus stand in parallel correspondence to the central joints *elbow* and *knee.*

This problem is missed often by persons with low IQs, although, like the previously examined figural reasoning item, it involves no obscure or unlikely perception.

If an examinee who answered *ankle* is informed that his choice is incorrect, he will most likely inspect the other alternatives and then guess another choice. If told not to guess but to think, he is lost; he stares in frustration and hops and skims over the problem abortively. He literally does not know how to think. He is unfamiliar and unpracticed in the analytical method that would lead him to select one alternative, view it in the combination *elbow-shoulder: knee-______*, and systematically search other information (in this case bodily structure) to explicate the relation. His shallow approach to reasoning is reminiscent of the inadequate discriminations and processing that poor word readers show before they have mastered the skills of phonic pronunciation, or that new drivers show while learning to drive.

Consider figural reasoning again to illustrate further the deficiency of low IQ. Directing a student with low IQ through a step-by-step analysis of a figural reasoning problem like the one presented as Figure 3 is often slow and difficult in a way that resembles the training of any new skill.

With one student, the instruction to compare the first two figures was not sufficient; he had to be explicitly asked to count the lines before he answered, "Two less lines." Then, when I asked him to compare the next two figures, he quickly replied, "Two less lines," although in this case only one line is deleted. Moreover, when he finished the last comparison, he did not carefully review the series to form an accurate rule, but quickly jumped to one of the wrong answers. This particular student was, by the way, an enterprising, fast-talking dope dealer in Berkeley before his arrest and later probation—a high school dropout with a test IQ of 85. He was anything but mentally dull. He was simply untutored in the procedures of detailed logical analysis.

A teacher or researcher seeking a fuller understanding of low IQ can obtain a first-hand view in the following manner. For the purpose of training adult intelligence, reading comprehension exercises are convenient. The deficient thinking habits characteristic of low IQ can be readily observed during the early phase of cognitive therapy when the student must continually be reminded to reread and reconsider sections of information he skipped and then further coaxed to combine the information in constructing the precise meaning of the material, rather than guessing at the meaning.

It should also be noted that, although I draw these observations from my own research, they are by no means original findings. Almost identical descriptions can be found in the writings of Bloom and Broder, Bereiter and Engelmann, and other researchers.

Let me digress for a moment to examine what appears to be a paradox: namely, that thoroughness leads to *quicker* solution of a problem. I have described the premature conclusion without sufficient thought that characterizes low IQ. When such a person takes a mathematics exam, he often finds himself incapable of arriving at a correct answer. Similarly, if he tries to do well on a verbal analogy test, and inspects all the alternatives before making a choice, he finds himself unable to choose one answer that is better than the others. He is not accomplished in the necessary steps. He does not systematically make various comparisons, nor does he search out and utilize all the information he possesses about the problem. And so he may sit in the testing room stubbornly challenging the problems, long after persons of high IQ have finished and left. He does not "catch on quickly" because he skims the problem material and his own thoughts hastily, instead of examining the details and the relations fully. The person of low IQ is not a slow thinker. When logical accuracy is not critical, as in light conversation and discussion, the individual with a low IQ may be quick and facile. He falters only when careful thought is required.

One more look at the mechanisms of intelligence is provided by an examination of reading comprehension.

Written verbal text is a symbolic representation of *relations* existing among objects and ideas. This is illustrated, for example, by the statement, "Paul is in the house and John is mowing the lawn." Easy reading—composed of short sentences and simple or familiar relations—does not require the fully developed skills of high intelligence. But trained attention to all the words and continuous analytical construction extending over lengthy verbal sequences are required in the comprehension of difficult text.

Errors of comprehension were illustrated in Chapter IV.

Here I shall illustrate the specific form intelligence takes in good reading. The last four sentences from the article on Greek culture quoted in Chapter IV are reproduced below:

> The comparison is no doubt dangerous, but can you imagine almost the entire population of an American city (in suitable installments, of course) sitting through performances of Mozart's *Don Giovanni* or Gluck's *Orpheus?* Perhaps the Athenian masses went to these plays because of a lack of other amusements. They could at least understand something of what went on, since the subjects were part of their folklore. For the American people, the subjects of grand opera are not part of their folklore.

Notice that in comprehending these sentences, you drew extensively on your own knowledge—not only of the meanings of words, but of other information, such as the absence of radio, television, and various amusements in ancient Greece. Furthermore, you carefully formed a mental replica of the ideas. But did you make any comparisons?

In figural reasoning, the activity of making comparisons is obvious. Comparisons are made, tentative subrelations are formed, further comparisons are made, the information is gathered together, and the overall rule is constructed. Similarly, in verbal analogy problems, comparisons are interspersed with constructions. However, in reading, comparative thinking is not as apparent.

Consider the sentence, "Perhaps the Athenian masses went to these plays because of a lack of other amusements." What is the writer saying? He is implying a comparison, and his meaning becomes clear only after the reader has completed the thought—Americans (in comparison with Greeks) may not attend the opera because (in comparison with Greeks) they have other sources of entertainment available to them. The writer does not, himself, make this statement about Americans. In fact, he jumps to an entirely different idea in the next sentence. The reader must complete the author's meaning by constructing the remainder of the comparison, or else miss his meaning. In complex reading material, ideas of comparison are often implied and require active construction by the reader.

Comparative thinking enters in another way. Notice that you followed the writer through a number of comparisons that were made in their entirety, such as the contrast between the content of Greek plays and of grand opera. Following comparisons in this way is facilitated for the reader with a high IQ by his own tendency to make analytical comparisons of situations. He has an easy familiarity with the direction taken by an author's comparative arguments—he is himself primed to classify elements in such a manner.

Self-initiated comparisons also play a major part in juxtaposing divergent opinions on a topic, in judging verity, and in checking one's grasp of an abstraction or generalization. Consider verity. In scrutinizing an author's argument, the examples and analogies he cites to support his position are compared point by point with his principal statements in order to confirm that they are truly pertinent and bear him out. The uses made of the same technical term in different parts of the argument are examined for consistency of meaning. Other examples and cases are called to mind—and collated with the writer's conclusions—in searching for contradictions to his assertions.

Checking and clarifying the meaning of broad or difficult propositions involve basically the same procedure. Specific examples are sought, compared, and matched with indefinite generalizations to dispel vagueness and base interpretations concretely. Bloom and Broder pointed out that the absence of this type of comparative analysis is a major flaw in the thinking of low-aptitude college students.

Finally, comparative thinking operates in answering the questions of a standard reading comprehension examination. The multiple-choice alternatives are compared with each other, and with the reading passage, in order to isolate the one that is most correct.

INTELLIGENCE AND REAL-LIFE PROBLEM SOLVING

Reading comprehension is a good starting point for resolving a difficulty that has plagued the psychometric concept of intelligence. Because the nature of intelligence was only partially understood until the intelligence-training studies complemented the picture obtained from psychometric data, psychometrists were hesitant to claim any more than that "intelligence is what intelligence tests measure." Yet, research study after research study showed that intelligence test scores reflect much more than this.

Reading comprehension is one expression of intelligence, and its primary importance in a literate-technical culture has been noted by many writers (for example, Miles Tinker). Lecture comprehension is a closely related expression of intelligence, with similarly obvious importance. Figure 4* illustrates the use of a combination of reading comprehension and arithmetic. Note how the skills of intelligence enter this problem. The meaning of, and the relation between, *all corporations* and *manufacturing corporations* must be fully interpreted in determining that the profits of *nonmanufacturing corporations* are computed from the difference. One low IQ examinee read $22 billion directly from the upper graph in answering the question, and chose alternative E. Without thorough analysis, he had regarded *all corporations* and *manufacturing corporations* as separate and nonoverlapping graphs, and had then jumped to the conclusion that *nonmanufacturing corporations* was simply the upper graph, since *manufacturing corporations* was the lower graph.

Another real-life expression of intelligence—discerning a

*From Turner (see Bibliography).

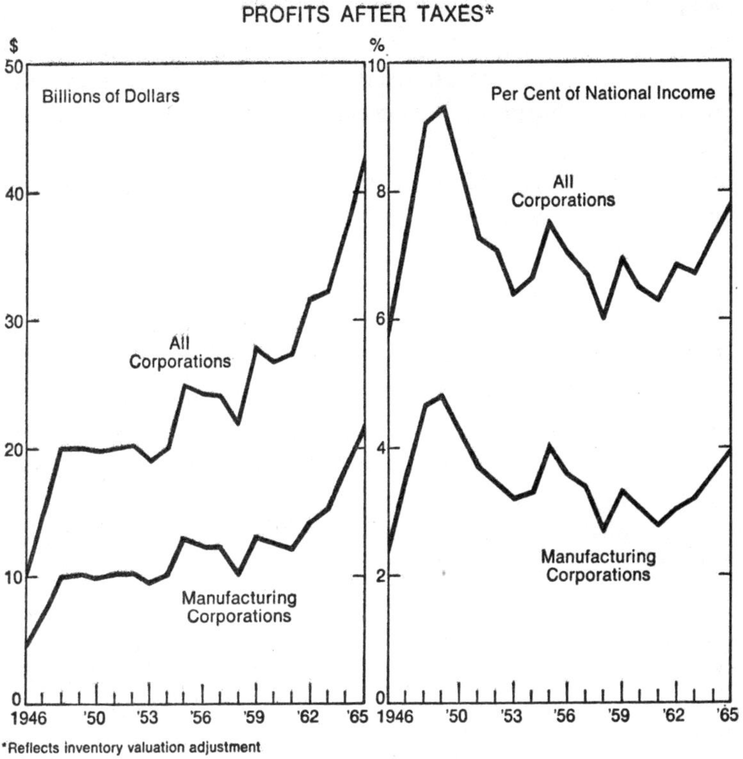

In 1958, the profit of *non*manufacturing corporations was:

A. $ 8 billion
B. $10 billion
C. $12 billion
D. $14 billion
E. none of the above

Figure 4. Sample Reading Comprehension and Arithmetic Problem. (From D. R. Turner, *Law School Admission Test,* New York: Anco, 1972) cause-and-effect *relation*—is the heart of scientific discovery and economic prediction and uses the mental skills of relation analysis.

Recall how a researcher discovers the *cause* of some phenomenon. He persistently compares and contrasts the exact details of the situations and events that precede several different occurrences of the phenomenon until he isolates the common and recurring antecedents. There is an obvious similarity between this process and, for example, figural reasoning.

The parallel between cause-and-effect problem solving (detailed observations, recall of prior knowledge, comparisons, and rule generation) and the activities involved in solving intelligence test items explains the broad validity of IQ tests. Tests such as figural reasoning, verbal analogy reasoning, and reading comprehension are miniature problem samples requiring the same thinking pattern that underlies scientific analysis, technical reasoning, and academic pursuits. "Intelligence" is an undeniably useful tool in life.

This is in no way contradicted by recent studies (such as that of Jencks, 1972) that have found only a moderate correlation between IQ and income in America. Motivation, interest in economic gain, minimum wage laws, and numerous other factors all attenuate the correlation. There is, however, no end to the number of studies that have demonstrated significant relations between intelligence test scores and academic achievement or occupational level (see Tyler, 1965). Table 2, for instance, presents estimated average IQs for different occupational levels, based on scores on the armed services induction test.

TABLE 2. OCCUPATIONAL LEVEL AND IQ

Occupation	*Average IQ*
Professional	120
Semiprofessional, managerial	113
Clerical, skilled trades, retail businessmen	108
Rural landowners, farmers	94
Semiskilled, minor clerical	104
Slightly skilled	96
Day laborers	95

SOURCE: *Johnson (see Bibliography)*

BINET'S CENSORSHIP OR AUTOCRITICISM

The definition of intelligence presented on page 120 emphasizes exactitude, which is implied by the terms *extensive, careful, thorough,* and *accurate.* Self-monitoring for accuracy has a special significance for intelligence because of the relatively long sequence of covert activities involved in reasoning and comprehension.

Many tasks of thought are immediately monitored by external feedback. For instance, steering an automobile through a turn is continuously guided by visual appraisal; errors of judgment do not wait upon completion of the entire maneuver, but are at once evident and demand correction. By contrast, in constructing the meaning of a reading passage or synthesizing a rule in figural reasoning, the entire process is internal and therefore unchecked save by self-censorship. Intelligence requires both a reflective approach to problems and constant reexamination and auditing for errors. In Binet's writings this is represented by the terms *censorship* and *auto-criticism.*

Shoddy, impulsive thought occurs repeatedly in the test responses and in the general thinking of examinees with low IQs. Bereiter and Engelmann, Bloom and Broder, and others have emphasized that imparting a concern, a value, for diligent accuracy is a prime function of cognitive therapy.

FULLY DEVELOPED INTELLECT

Reading comprehension, figural reasoning, mathematical reasoning, and other expressions of intelligence all involve an extended sequence of observation, searches for information, comparisons, and constructions. Particularizing the mental activities in this explicit manner, however, does not mean that initiation and control are continuously at the center of consciousness. On the contrary, intelligence tends to operate in the quasi-automatic manner characteristic of all skilled behaviors. Fitts and Posner (1967) have given us a picture of this process in the case of a physical skill:

> During the early phase of skill learning it is usually necessary to attend to cues, events, and responses that later go unnoticed. In learning a dance step, one attends to kinesthetic and visual information about the feet, information which is later ignored.

In the same vein, Simon and Chase have described the advanced chess player as gathering and processing game-relevant information in a somewhat automatic or habitual manner:

> The empirical data from human subjects indicate that . . . the player sets himself (not necessarily consciously or deliberately, but perhaps habitually) the task of acquiring information about the chess-significant relations on the board.

In the case of intelligence, this same process is illustrated by the change in mental habit that occurs over the course of cognitive therapy (as indicated, for example, by Bereiter and Engelmann).

In the early stages of cognitive therapy the impulse to seek understanding, to apprehend and combine facts into relations, must be intentionally initiated and regularly monitored lest it be neglected. Furthermore, the novice is awkward and confused, much like a student driver; he may let facts slip and have difficulty following a long sequence of thought because he too readily skims his mind and thereby loses the full train of ideas, details, and connections.

Gradually, however, the mental pattern of intelligence—a perceptual orientation to seek and construct relations continually while proceeding through material—becomes quasi-automatic. In fact, when intelligence is deeply ingrained, it is often unnecessary consciously to review and reiterate the earlier ideas of a reasoning problem or a verbal argument in integrating each new element of information. Instead, the earlier relations are stored in memory as active, continually developing mental sets or frames of reference that cue the mind for the interpretation of subsequent material. In this way they form a comparative context, which by its very nature effects analysis and integration. The process is parallel to the thinking of an experienced driver when he notes some traffic condition, such as the position of another automobile seen in the rear view mirror. The information does not dominate his consciousness—he may, for example, continue in a conversation he was having—yet it sets the context of subsequent decisions and guides his driving until the condition has passed.

The term *quasi-automatic* needs some additional comment to clarify the nature of intelligence. A skill well-learned does not require total and constant attention; for example, an experienced driver can engage in conversation while driving. The detailed behaviors of the skill seem to attain a certain quality of habitualness, almost an autonomy, so that only partial or indirect attention is required for continued performance. Yet, no degree of mastery can completely untether a skill from intention or motivation; a skill never becomes fully automatic—it becomes only quasi-automatic. This continued dependence on volition is manifested in two ways. First, skilled performance is at its best when given full attention, when competent fluency wrought of practice and experience is amplified by conscious direction. Second, skills never become fully autonomous: When motivation ceases so does performance.

Driving an automobile serves again to illustrate the first point. An experienced driver can engage in conversation or personal thought, and drive in an off-hand, second-nature manner. But in bad weather or heavy traffic, he brings extra care and concentration to the job. Similarly, as he draws near his trip's end, especially if he seeks a street or a highway exit that is easily missed, he consciously decides to give more attention to road signs and less attention to conversation.*

Tasks of intelligence show similar gradations of conscious intent. Easy reading, for example, can proceed without the fullest intensity of concentration. But when the material is important and involved, full wits are gathered to the task. At such time, pivotal sentences and thoughts may be repeated and reexamined with the deliberateness that is required of a student in cognitive therapy, but with far greater profit owing to better developed skill. In reading and reflection, as in driving, skilled performance is most effective with total convergence of thought.

A skill never becomes fully automatic in the sense of not requiring continuous motivation. Consider, for example, tying shoelaces—certainly among the simplest of skills. Tying

*Essentially this corresponds to the "serial processing" notion of Newell and Simon (1972, p. 89) and the "single-channel" hypothesis of other researchers in the area of human performance and information processing.

shoelaces is done by an adult in an ostensibly automatic manner. But let him become deeply involved in conversation, or distracted by a shocking news report, and shoe lacing may taper off, forgotten. When motivation shifts, the seemingly automatic behavior ceases.

In a selection quoted earlier, Sir Frederick Bartlett noted that every kind of bodily skill is "used for the attempted achievement of whatever issue may be required at the time of the performance," and similarly, every kind of thinking is "used in an attempt to satisfy some requirement of the occasion upon which the thinking takes place." Just as a skill is always directed toward some objective, so it is invoked only when there is a motivation for its exercise. There is a common misconception that intelligent responses are made naturally and automatically by intelligent people. This is no more true than the idea that driving occurs naturally in good drivers. If motivation to drive actually ceased in mid-trip, the automobile would slow to a stop or perhaps veer from the road.

Undoubtedly good drivers approach their vehicles with an attitude of properly going about the business of driving. Similarly, intelligent persons tend to bring their skills of analysis to the business of life. But it is important to stress that intelligence in a particular area falters unless supported by the impulse to comprehend and master. This fact explains many inconsistencies where, owing to capricious motivation, a person shows high intelligence in one area but confusion and error in another. Fostering the desire to comprehend is the first step in training intelligence. Intellectual production or creation is invariably motivated by a strong drive to fully comprehend and organize some area of knowledge. Albert Einstein, for example, in describing his own thinking, said: "It is also clear that the desire to arrive finally at logically connected concepts is the emotional basis of this [mental activity]."*

*From a letter written by Einstein to the French mathematician, Hadamard (1945).

Recognition that the intelligent grasp and solution of a difficult question does not occur full-blown and without persistent, directed thinking is essential to a complete understanding of mental capacity. All too often the person with low IQ feels that in order to maintain his self-esteem he must arrive at the answer to a problem instantaneously. Quite the contrary. All the activities described in Chapter IV as contributing to good comprehension—subvocalization, visualization, returning to and reexamining earlier parts of the material, and, especially, gradual, diligent construction of relationships—apply to the solution of any and all puzzles posed to the mind.

INTELLIGENCE, NEUROLOGICAL CORRELATES, AND GENETICS

The attentional/processing skill definition of intelligence is only one dimension of a complete theory of mental capacity. Analyses of intelligence that focus on neurological correlates of skilled thinking will contribute additional perspectives to our understanding. Recognizing the neurological correlates of intelligence is not inconsistent with searching for techniques to train intelligence. Studies have already shown that some neurological functions, such as the alpha pattern, can be changed through training. Moreover, there is an expanding body of research, with both animals and humans, showing the effects of an organism's prenatal and postnatal experiences on its neurological activities. Eventually this research will be integrated with training studies of the type summarized in Chapter III.

Viewing intelligence as a skill does not preclude the possibility that genetic factors can influence its development and expression. It is quite possible that under certain conditions all skills are characterized by a determinable heritability. Nevertheless, regarding intelligence as a skill centers attention on the potential efficacy of structured training.

The intelligence-training studies described in Chapter III will hopefully spark a large-scale attack on the problem of finding feasible methods for teaching thinking skills to all students.

VI. THE GENETICS OF INTELLIGENCE

A primary deterrent to the development of intelligence-training methods has been the belief that human intelligence is largely genetically determined and, therefore, not subject to improvement. A widely popularized statement of this belief—that *80 percent of the variance in intelligence is genetically determined, with 20 percent contributed by environment*—has been vocally championed by Arthur Jensen, of the University of California at Berkeley, in numerous articles, in his hotly debated paper in the *Harvard Educational Review,* and in a recent book.

The statement is, in an important sense, a textbook example of lying with statistics. This condemnation does not imply any intended deception on Jensen's part: The lie is a matter of methodological orientation. However, it has been quoted by Jensen, Richard Herrnstein, William Shockley, and other genetic determinists to support their arguments that innate differences in intelligence exist among the races and that bringing higher education to the lower socioeconomic classes is an impossible task.* Yet the statement is basically an oversimplification of the experimental data, arising from a narrow

*Jensen and Shockley have maintained that genetically based racial and social class differences exist in IQ. By contrast, Herrnstein argues only that social class disparities in IQ are genetically founded. Herrnstein has insisted that any conclusion about racial differences is premature. He has written: "Cultural factors, general surroundings, and racial discrimination complicate the analysis in unknown ways."

statistical perspective, and it greatly distorts the true influence environment does have and can have on intelligence.

The 80 percent and 20 percent values were arrived at by studying the correspondences and similarities between the intelligence test scores of relatives: father-son, brother-sister, uncle-nephew, grandfather-grandson, etc. All these comparisons suffer the limitation that it is impossible to separate fully the factor of similar environment—of living together or being members of the same social family and culture—from purely genetic influences. The comparison that, until recently, has been regarded as freest of this criticism—and that is most often cited—is the comparison of identical twins raised separately. There exist four studies of this type: one performed in the United States (Newman, Freeman, and Holzinger, 1937), two in England (Burt, 1966; Shields, 1962), and one in Denmark (Juel-Nielsen, 1965).

At a recent meeting of the Eastern Psychological Association, Leon Kamin, of Princeton, pointed to a number of serious flaws in the separated-twins studies.*

First, the twins in these "life experiments" were not randomly placed into homes that sampled the entire range of societal conditions. Adoption agencies screen families, so there is a tendency for the adoptive families to be of a similar type. Furthermore, there is often an attempt to match adoptive families to children's characteristics. In addition, the reports of both Burt's and Shields's studies indicate that the twins often remained within the same geographical locale, shared similar religious and social customs, and in a few cases actually lived within the same community and knew each other. All these factors contribute to a reduction and underestimation of the proportion of IQ variance attributable to environment.

Second, in Shields's study, Shields himself tested *both* twins in 33 of his 38 pairs. Thus the double-blind testing

*Norman Daniels (1973) has reviewed Kamin's analysis. The present synopsis is drawn from the works of both writers.

procedure was not used and experimenter bias had an opportunity to intrude. The data, in fact, indicate that such intrusion occurred. For the 33 twin pairs tested by Shields, the average IQ difference was 4.9 points. In the 5 instances where Shields tested one twin and his assistant tested the other, the average IQ difference was 13.2 points. The latter difference is close to what would be expected if heredity plays only a small role in determining intelligence. Burt, apparently, also administered most of the tests himself, so the data from his study were also subject to unconscious bias.

A third difficulty noted by Kamin is that IQ test standardization is often age-dependent. (In other words, the IQs of persons who differ in age cannot be directly compared.) Since the various twin pairs differed in age, a spuriously high correlation was produced. Kamin showed that in at least one study, the correlation between separated twins can be accounted for almost entirely by the lack of age standardization.

Kamin made the fourth and most serious charge against Burt's study. Burt's is the largest of the four investigations and the one cited most frequently by hereditarians. Apparently Burt did not use standardized IQ tests in all instances. In a footnote he spoke of giving "personal interviews" and "camouflaged IQ tests." Furthermore, Burt made "adjusted assessments" in some cases; there are discrepancies of experimental data between Burt's report and that published by his assistant; the original data sheets have been destroyed so they cannot be examined; and there is even a strong suggestion that some of the statistical computations have been fudged.

All in all, Kamin's analysis has cast serious doubt on the usefulness of the four separated-twins studies reported in the literature. Additional, more carefully controlled studies are needed to evaluate the true correlation between separated twins. In fact, the Eastern Psychological Association (to whom Kamin presented his criticisms) voted to "censure the use of inconclusive evidence concerning the heritability of IQ."

But there is a broader point at issue in regarding the

80:20 ratio as a statistical lie. The logic of correlating test scores of relatives is theoretically unsuited for evaluating the potency that training and other environmental factors do have and can have in influencing intelligence. A detailed examination of the American study of separated twins illustrates this unsuitability.

THE INTERPRETATION OF IQ SCORE CORRELATIONS

Over the course of several years, Horatio Newman, Frank Freeman, and Karl Holzinger were able to locate 19 pairs of identical twins who for sundry reasons grew up in different households. The twins' Stanford-Binet IQs were measured and are listed in Table 3.

The experimenters computed the correlation of these scores to be .67 (perfect correlation is +1.00) and a further statistical manipulation called analysis of variance yielded the conclusion that 69 percent of the *statistical* score variance of these data was genetically determined and 31 percent was environmentally determined.

Now 69:31 is a little below the 80:20 ratio cited by Jensen. Christopher Jencks (in *Inequality*) noted that in all the studies of relatives, estimates of genetic influence based on American samples run lower than those based on British samples, perhaps attributable to greater environmental diversity in the United States. The 80:20 ratio is really an average of the American and European data pooled.

The mathematical details of computing the 69:31 estimate need not concern us here—the interested reader can find a full discussion of various procedures in Jencks's book. Here we shall examine the data from another perspective.

The really important question is: "What does the .67 correlation mean?" It means simply that if one twin of a pair has a high IQ, the other one also *tends* to be above average; and if one is below average, the other also tends to be low.

TABLE 3.
STANFORD-BINET IQS OF IDENTICAL TWINS SEPARATED IN INFANCY

Pair	*Twin 1*		*Twin 2*
A	85		97
B	66		78
C	99		101
D	89	←—17—→	106
E	89		93
F	102		94
G	105		106
H	92		77
I	102		96
J	122		127
K	92	←—24—→	116
L	116		109
M	94		95
N	85		84
O	91		90
P	90		88
Q	115		105
R	96	←—19—→	77
S	88		79

Adapted from Newman, Freeman, and Holzinger (1937).

Perusal of Table 3 shows this to be true: Twins B are both quite low, twins J are both high. There are exceptions to the trend, however. Twins K, for example, have a 24-point separation in their IQs, and two other pairs (R and D) have 19 and 17 point differences, respectively. Such large IQ differences between *genetic duplicates* cannot be ignored; yet, that is exactly what the Jensen-type statistical review does. It looks only at the general trend and conceals the important exceptions. An IQ difference of 20 points is in fact enormous. It represents, for example, the contrast between an individual whose academic limit is mediocre high school grades, and one who completes college easily.

The original experimenters, Newman et al., explored this point further. For each pair of separated twins, they rated the contrast in the educational backgrounds provided by the respective foster homes and found that these disparities correlated highly ($r=.79$) with IQ differences: Identical twins with discrepant IQs were raised under educationally dissimilar conditions; those with close IQs had similar educational backgrounds. For instance, twins K, the twins with the largest IQ disparity, had also been the subject of the sharpest contrast in educational opportunity. Their scholastic histories were summarized by Newman et al. as follows:

> Helen's second foster-mother, though having had few educational advantages herself, was determined that the foster-daughter should have every educational opportunity, and stood out for her convictions against the opposition of the foster-father, who considered higher education for women as nonsense. Helen never was required really to work on the farm, though when at home she assisted with the housework.
>
> Helen took a Bachelor's degree from a good Michigan college and soon afterward became a schoolteacher, first in a small town and for the last eight years in a large school in Detroit. She has taught principally English and history but has had to fill in her time with a variety of other subjects, including dancing. Her work has been confined to the middle grades. On the whole, her educational experience as student and teacher has been extensive.
>
> Gladys was much less fortunate in her educational opportunities. She went to the Rocky Mountains when she was about ready to go into third grade. During the next two years no school was available, and after her return to Ontario she was probably too old to associate comfortably with third-graders, for she was twelve years old at that time. The result was that she never went back to school. Thus, there was a very marked contrast—the greatest found in any of our cases—between the

extensive education of Helen and the nearly total lack of formal education of Gladys.

Newman et al. also observed that the differences in IQ, resulting from the divergent educational experiences, could not be attributed solely to a greater accumulation of specific facts and bits of academic knowledge. Basic analytical reasoning ability appeared to have improved as well:

> That the superiority . . . cannot be ascribed merely to the possession of information . . . is shown by an analysis of the test scores. The International Test, which is a nonlanguage test, and does not include materials taught in school, yields . . . [some] of the largest differences. Many of the tests of the Stanford-Binet Scale . . . utilize materials which are not to be found in the school. School work can be thought to prepare for the passing of these tests only on the assumption that the mental operations which are required in passing them are facilitated by the work of the school. Examples of such tests are the "ball and field" test, requiring one to trace the path he would follow to find a ball lost in a circular field; . . . and the "code" test, requiring one to translate a sentence into a simple code made of lines and figures.

A strong contrast in intellectual growth incentive was likewise seen in the case of twins R, whose IQs differed by 19 points:

> These twins, twenty-seven years old, were born in a mountain village in southeastern Tennessee. The mother died in childbirth. The father, a coal miner, managed to keep the twins for a time, but, when he remarried less than a year after his first wife died, the twins' grandparents took the infants, James going to the maternal and Reece to the paternal grandparents. Because of strained relations between the two foster-families, the twins have never associated. In fact, their visit to Chicago was the first time they had spent more than a few hours together.

James's grandparents are people of steady and industrious character. His grandfather and his maternal uncle have lived in a small town and have operated a sawmill and a sand-and-gravel business. James has been for nearly ten years employed as engineer in this business. The grandfather had never received much education but was very "good at figures." The uncle seems to be a man of superior ability and character and seems to have had a very steadying influence on James. This family is considered as rather well to do in the small community. James seems to be very greatly interested in machinery, especially in boat engines and dredging machinery, and is considered more or less of an expert along those lines. He has been steadily employed ever since he was graduated from high school. . . .

Reece was reared by his paternal grandparents. . . . This family is one of a type common in the mountains of Tennessee. They are regular mountaineers of the more primitive sort. The grandfather had never worked steadily but had tried his hand at coalmining, blacksmithing, and work on the railroad. He was a Confederate veteran, and his pension was almost enough to live on, so steady work was not essential. He lived to be ninety years old. Both grandparents could read and write, but that was the extent of their intellectual attainments. Reece has followed the custom of the family in avoiding regular work. He has had very few jobs. For a short time he worked in an automobile factory, but this was "too much like slavery" to him, so he returned to the mountains. It would not be fair to recount in this place any of his less creditable occupations and experiences. Suffice it to say that his whole life has had a totally different tenor from that of James. . . .

James completed grade school and high school in a town of about two thousand inhabitants. He was moderately interested in his studies, enjoying science and mathematics but disliking English. He was a member of the high school football team but did not care for the milder sports. Since boyhood he has shown great interest in machinery of all sorts and has done some reading along those lines. He also reads history and historical novels.

Reece attended a mountain school when he felt so inclined, but never for more than five months in the year, usually much less. He continued, however, through the eighth grade. He liked arithmetic and history but disliked English. He has no pleasant memories of school. It is obvious that Reece has had educational advantages far inferior to those of James.

Arthur Jensen, in his *Harvard Educational Review* paper "How Much Can We Boost IQ and Scholastic Achievement?" has neglected to mention discrepant cases of this type that form the exceptions to the statistical analysis he does report. But, in fact, it is the exceptions that prove the rule: Environment has a powerful effect on intelligence, much more so than the 80:20 ratio would suggest. In particular, these case studies show that environmental and cultural factors could easily account for the observed racial and social class IQ differences (in every instance less than 15 IQ points) that Jensen and Shockley have been so quick to ascribe to genetic origins.

Consider now the second phase of the position taken by Jensen and other genetic determinists. Armed with the correlations between family members, they have argued against the utility of instituting programs for training intelligence. But suppose a genetic correlation was found to exist in driving ability. It is quite possible, for instance, that similarities of identical twins in temperament, personality, physical coordination, and psychomotor abilities could produce some parallel in accident rate. Would this mean that formal driving instruction should be discontinued, that federal appropriations for highway safety programs should be cut? A more dramatic example can be drawn from the history of medicine: Susceptibility to tuberculosis appears to have a genetic component causing the disease to occur in a familial pattern. But improved medical knowledge and public health measures have reduced the incidence of tuberculosis enormously, showing the effectiveness of an intervention program.

The expression (or phenotype) taken by any genotype always depends on the environment in which it develops;

geneticists refer to this as the genetic-by-environment interaction. Put simply, the statistical demonstration that genes *can* influence intelligence is not really relevant to the question of how operative environmental intervention or training might be. A study on animal learning by R.M. Cooper and John Zubek suggests that genetic factors in intelligence would disappear completely if training were instituted on a wide scale. An estimate like the 80:20 ratio is at best an actuarial description of status quo, a gross summary of momentarily existing conditions. In the time since Jensen popularized the 80:20 value, a number of biologists (such as Lewontin, 1970) have pointed out that such a percentage estimate is meaningless in an absolute sense and that it could change drastically with an alteration of prevalent educational methods. In fact, in the opening pages of his *Harvard Educational Review* paper, Jensen himself defined the limits to which his conclusions apply, although he failed to recognize the possibility of certain educational changes:

> The instructional methods of the traditional classroom were not invented all in one stroke, but evolved within an upper-class segment of the European population, and thus were naturally shaped by the capacities, culture, and needs of those children whom the schools were primarily intended to serve. At least implicit in the system as it originally developed was the expectation that not all children would succeed. These methods of schooling have remained essentially unchanged for many generations. We have accepted traditional instruction so completely that it is extremely difficult even to imagine, much less to put into practice, any radically different forms that the education of children could take. Our thinking almost always takes for granted such features as beginning formal instruction at the same age for all children (universally between ages five and six), instruction of children in groups, keeping the same groups together in lock-step fashion through the first several years of schooling, and an active-passive, showing-seeing, telling-listening relationship between teacher and pupils. Satisfactory learn-.

> ing occurs under these conditions only when children come to school with certain prerequisite abilities and skills: an attention span long enough to encompass the teacher's utterances and demonstrations, the ability voluntarily to focus one's attention where it is called for, the ability to comprehend verbal utterances and to grasp relationships between things and their symbolic representations, the ability to inhibit large-muscle activity and engage in covert "mental" activity, to repeat instruction to oneself, to persist in a task until a self-determined standard is attained—in short, the ability to engage in what might be called self-instructional activities, without which group instruction alone remains ineffectual.

Until recently very little research had been done on the problem of using either group or individual instruction to develop "the ability to engage in self-instructional activities."

Exploring the chemical components of the genes that *may* influence intellectual aptitude might be an interesting research project for biochemists and neurophysiologists. But the task of education is to isolate the set of environmental conditions that maximizes the development of academic aptitude or intelligence—and then to provide these conditions to all children. Jensen's purblind 80:20 statistic does its greatest damage in discouraging research and social progress of this type.

EXPERIMENTS IN EUGENICS AND EUTHENICS

All imaginable correlations and comparisons of the intelligence test scores of relatives have been computed. However, researchers have differed in the way they analyze such data. In *Inequality,* Christopher Jencks used a somewhat different statistical procedure than that used by Jensen and concluded that the proportion of intelligence attributable to genetics is 40 percent—perhaps even as low as 20 percent if errors of estimation are taken into account. However, this statement is still ambiguous and easily misinterpreted. There remains the question of exactly how the correlations arise—what the underlying mechanisms are. In the final analysis, the avalanche of family relation correlation data can provide no more than circumstantial evidence regarding the heritability of IQ. Primary eugenics research with humans is precluded by social and moral constraints. Animal researchers, however, have made a direct attack on the issue.

In 1929, Robert Tryon, at Berkeley, attempted to develop strains of "bright" and "dull" (his terms) rats through selective breeding. He used a T-maze to measure rat intelligence, and bred high scorers to other high scorers, and lows to lows. After eight generations, Tryon had two distinct subpopulations that differed markedly in maze performance: Members of the high-scoring group ran the maze more quickly and made fewer errors. He had apparently bred for intelligence.

But the study did not end there. Another Berkeley researcher, Lloyd Searle, explored some further questions. Was the bright strain more intelligent in a *general* sense, and were there additional dimensions on which the bright and dull rats differed? To investigate the first point, Searle tested the two strains on a number of other standard laboratory measures of rat learning, measures that differed in various ways from the original T-maze used by Tryon. These included, for example, an elevated maze (which did not have enclosing walls like the T-maze, but consisted of a path of thin wooden strips supported in the air, thus allowing and requiring the use of a different set of cues for solving and traversing the maze), an underwater maze, and a Lashley jumping stand discrimination apparatus. In contrast to the persisting superiority of the bright strain on the original T-maze used for selective breeding, the bright rats did not surpass the dull rats on the other learning tests. In some cases the dull rats actually scored higher. To probe further, the rats were given "personality" tests—contrivances that measured motivation, emotionality, and activity rather than learning. The picture that emerged was summarized in Searle's concluding remarks:

> No evidence was found that a difference exists between the Brights and Dulls in the learning capacity per se. A detailed study of the behavior profiles indicated that Brights are characteristically food-driven, economical of distance, low in motivation to escape from water, and timid in response to open spaces. Dulls are relatively disinterested in food, average or better in water motivation, and timid of mechanical apparatus. It is concluded that brightness and dullness in the original Tryon Maze may be accounted for in large part by such motivational and emotional patterns.

Thus in an actual eugenics experiment, one in which social learning and cultural differences did not confound the interpretation, there was no evidence for the genetic dictation of intelligence. On the contrary, strain differences in manifest intelligence were the product of emotional and motivational factors.

Other experiments showing motivational differences between bright and dull rats have been summarized by John Fuller and Robert Thompson (1960). Furthermore, Searle's conclusions have been confirmed by John Scott and Margaret Charles (1953), who studied the learning abilities of various breeds of dogs. They reported (as cited by Hayes, 1962) that in dogs

> important innately caused differences in performance are produced by differences in emotional, motivational and peripheral processes, and . . . genetically caused differences in central [intellectual] processes may be either slight or non-existent.

Jensen has compared variations in human mentality to the structural characteristics of automobiles. A person with a low IQ, attempting a mental test problem, is like a Volkswagen struggling up a steeply graded hill; a person with a high IQ is like a powerful Mercedes, which is built with a better capacity for the task. Searle's results suggest a different model: namely, that human brains are like identical computers, which all have exactly the same hardware or neural equipment, but which are programed for solving different types of problems. Humans differ in their cognitive orientations—because they are dissimilar in goals, values, and approaches to life.

With rats, genetic factors exert their influence on mentality through motivational channels. Hayes (1962) has proposed that human intellect is structured in a similar manner. Humans, he has suggested, are equal in innate learning ability but are genetically different in motives and drives. Certain of these drives, which he termed experience-producing drives (EPDs), result in exposure to specific types of learning experiences and the development of corresponding cognitive abilities. As a hypothetical example, Hayes submitted that a strong "speech drive" might lead to acquisition of vocabulary, word fluency, reading ability, and other verbal skills.

There is longitudinal evidence from the Fels Research Institute that motives are related to intellectual growth (Sontag, Baker, and Nelson, 1958; Kagan, Sontag, Baker, and Nelson, 1958). Children's IQs were periodically measured for the first 12 years of life. Children whose IQs increased tended to score high on rating scales reflecting *interests in activities* (such as a scale labeled General Competitiveness); they also showed more Achievement Imagery and Themes of Curiosity about Nature on the Thematic Apperception Test (TAT). But as yet there is no evidence that such drives are innate in humans. Moreover, as Hayes noted, with animals plentiful data indicate that the activity drive and other motives are highly subject to environmental alteration. For example, a study I conducted with Victor Denenberg (1966) showed that psychometric-type patterns of individual differences in the curiosity, emotionality, and activity of rats—patterns previously regarded as largely genetic—could be generated through the programing of early life experiences. Denenberg's book, *The Development of Behavior,* has summarized a host of studies in the area. One of these studies (Cooper and Zubek, 1958) showed that even in a relatively primitive animal like the rat, any genetic control that does exist evidently has a very tenuous grip on cognitive processes.

Cooper and Zubek began with strains of rats that had been bred to be bright or dull. Experimental subgroups of each strain were then selected to spend their adolescence (25 through 65 days of age) in one of three laboratory conditions. One pair of subgroups—a bright subgroup and a dull subgroup—was placed in an *enriched* environment consisting of modernistically painted cages with mirrors, swings, ramps, polished balls, marbles, barriers, slides, tunnels, bells, teeter-totters, and springboards. A second pair of subgroups was raised in the *normal* laboratory environment. And a third pair went into a *restricted* environment where darkened empty cages were surrounded by uniformly gray walls.

Subsequent to this the maze learning of all six groups was tested. The animals brought up under *normal* laboratory conditions exhibited the typical pattern: Bright rats made fewer maze errors than dull rats. But the *restricted* environment changed this. Impoverished stimulation had a deleterious effect on the capacity of the bright rats: They grew up dull and were as poor in learning as the dull strain. The *enriched* environment had just the opposite effect. The dull rats benefited from the wealth of stimulation: Their cognitive patterns were altered, they flourished, and their learning capacity was fully equal to that of the bright rats. The dulls were no longer dull.

These results, in conjunction with Searle's interpretation of his own findings, indicate that measured learning capacity is the final stage in a complicated developmental process. Many factors are operative; innate propensity is but one rather remote contributor. The distinguishing characteristic of *Homo sapiens* is plasticity: Ideologies, beliefs, and learned motives of survival (Miller, 1948) all have an overriding influence in molding human behavior. Formal education has left the growth of thinking skills largely to chance; only in primitive and uncultivated ground do congenital factors find a clear path of expression. Where the educational system has improved

IQ, it has (as Bereiter put it) done so "inadvertently." Cooper and Zubek's data, the large IQ discrepancies between some identical twins, and results of studies such as the Wisconsin Project (Chapter III) all suggest that explicit training would completely inundate any small trickle of influence genetics can have on intelligence.*

HUMAN POPULATION TRENDS

A significant body of evidence that argues against the notion that IQ is genetically determined comes from the study of changes in intelligence test scores occurring over successive generations. Periodically, behavioral scientists have predicted a drastic plunge in human intelligence. This prediction is based on two facts. First, persons from the lower socioeconomic classes tend to score poorly on IQ tests; and second, the lower classes tend to have larger families (United Nations, 1955). Presumably, then, since persons of low mental ability reproduce in greater numbers than those of high mental ability, an overall drop in average IQ would result.

Certain statistical considerations complicate predictions of this sort (Anastasi, 1956; Hunt, 1961), but these need not concern us here. More important is the fact that *all* the studies in the area have shown just the opposite to be true: Average IQ is on the rise.

For example, Raymond B. Cattell in 1937 multiplied IQ scores by the reproduction rates of people at various IQ levels and on this basis predicted that the average IQ of the following generation would be lower. Several years later, Cattell tested his prediction. He compared the average IQ of 10-year-olds in Leicester, England, in 1949 with the average IQ of 10-year-olds in the same city in 1936. He found that an in-

*Experiments by Fleishman and Hempel (1954, 1955) demonstrate that the factors which affect a skilled performance are altered drastically over the course of learning. Characteristics that are important when little or no training exists may have no influence whatever after a period of training.

crease rather than a decrease in IQ had occurred during the period.

As another example, records show that the average score made by World War II inductees on the Army Alpha Test was significantly higher than the average score made by their World War I counterparts (Tuddenham, 1948). The World War II median was, in fact, at the 82nd percentile of the World War I distribution. Researchers have interpreted this to mean that between 1914 and 1940 there was a gain in the national average IQ, brought about by an increase and improvements in American educational facilities.

To cite one more case, S. Smith measured the IQ of children in various schools in Honolulu in 1924 and again in 1938. Not only did the children show a 10-point increase in verbal IQ, but they gained an estimated 20 points on a nonverbal IQ test composed of Maze Tracing, Copying Figures, and Figure Classification. It is significant that these nonverbal subtests are not directly dependent on academic content; instead they reflect general thinking capacity. A number of other studies have shown similar results, all suggesting that intelligence is a learned human capacity, the development of which is encouraged by a society's technological and educational advances.

GENETIC ABNORMALITY

Genetic abnormalities are a common source of confusion in discussions of the relation between genetics and mental capacity. Mongolism, or Downs' syndrome, is a congenital dysfunction characterized by slanted eyes, a small head, diminutive stature, greatly shortened life span, and acute mental deficiency. Mongoloids are born with 47 chromosomes instead of the normal 46, and this abnormality causes physiological disruption. Since chromosomes contain the genetic material, this pathological condition is an indisputable case of genetically based mental retardation.

In many minds mongolism has served implicitly as a model for the belief that all intelligence is genetically determined. This is an erroneous conceptual leap. Mongolism is a distinct disease syndrome, not a downward extension of normal healthy intelligence. Consider an analogy to another form of mental retardation.

Severe thyroid deficiency in early life produces a type of feeblemindedness called cretinism. Unlike mongolism, cretinism has no known genetic origin. However, one might speculate that because in this instance thyroid dysfunction disrupts intelligence, thyroid hormone production is related to IQ differences across the entire range of mental ability. But such a hypothesis has found no empirical support. Studies carried out with adolescents (Shock and Jones, 1939) and with college students (summarized by Yarbrough and McCurdy, 1958) showed absolutely no correlation between thyroid indices and intelligence. We cannot, on the basis of the relation between cretinism and thyroid activity conclude that the thyroid gland influences variations of normal IQ. Analogously, the fact that mongolism, a genetically based disorder, is associated with mental deficiency does not argue for the importance of genetic endowment in producing the variations of intellectual ability found among normal adults.

A victim of Downs' syndrome is afflicted with slurred speech, difficulty in counting and elementary arithmetic, greatly restricted memory span, and complete incapacity for skills such as driving. By contrast, the healthy individual with a low IQ may be articulate, knowledgeable in life, skilled in a vocation, an interesting friend, and a witty companion—all reflecting the intact and wholesome condition of his neural functions. His deficiency is of a specific, isolated type, and there is absolutely no scientific reason to assume that his neurons, glial cells, DNA, RNA, acetylcholine, cholinesterase, reverberating circuits, or other aspects of his mental chemistry are in any way genetically inferior.

In his *Harvard Educational Review* paper, Arthur Jensen

fell into exactly the logical trap we have just considered. He used a genetic aberration to support his contention that genes play a significant role in determining the differences in mental capacity found among normal adults. Under the easily misconstrued subtitle, "Direct Evidence of Genetic Influences on Human Abilities," he argued:

> One of the most striking pieces of evidence for the genetic control of mental abilities is a chromosomal anomaly called Turner's syndrome. Normal persons have 46 chromosomes. Persons with Turner's syndrome have only 45. When their chromosomes are stained and viewed under the microscope, it is seen that the sex-chromatin is missing from one of the two chromosomes that determine the individual's sex. In normal persons this pair of chromosomes is conventionally designated XY for males and XX for females. The anomaly of Turner's syndrome is characterized as XO. These persons always have the morphologic appearance of females but are always sterile, and they show certain physical characteristics such as diminutive stature, averaging about five feet tall as adults. The interesting point about Turner's cases from our standpoint is that although their IQs on most verbal tests of intelligence show a perfectly normal distribution, their performance on tests involving spatial ability or perceptual organization is abnormally low (Money, 1964). Their peculiar deficiency in spatial-perceptual ability is sometimes so severe as to be popularly characterized as "space-form blindness." It is also interesting that Turner's cases seem to be more or less uniformly low on spatial ability regardless of their level of performance on other tests of mental ability. These rare persons also report unusual difficulty with arithmetic and mathematics in school despite otherwise normal or superior intelligence. So here is a genetic aberration, clearly identifiable under the microscope, which has quite specific consequences on cognitive processes. Such specific intellectual deficiencies are thus entirely possible without there being any specific environmental deprivations needed to account for them.
>
> There are probably other more subtle cognitive effects associated with the sex chromosomes in normal persons.

Following this description, Jensen launched into a hypothetical discussion of how genes might influence all aspects of intelligence. But the supposedly focal evidence turns out to be a conceptual error in which he has drawn a conclusion about normal cognitive development from evidence that is obviously peculiar to an abnormal genetic condition.

Apparently the full complement of 46 chromosomes is necessary for physical and mental growth to progress in a normal, nonpathological fashion. But except in a small number of disease conditions involving both physical and mental symptoms, little can be said about the relation between genetic chemistry and intellectual functioning. In view of Kamin's methodological criticisms of the separated-twins studies, the supposition that genes play a strong role in affecting variations of normal intelligence is, at the present time, very much open to question.

VII.

RACE AND

IQ

Throughout this book evidence has been presented that IQ is related to perceptual habit, cognitive orientation, home and school learning, and values. Thus average IQ varies with social class. At present no definitive evidence warrants the conclusion that IQ is biologically related to race.

Black, brown, red, white, and yellow persons of middle-class background are basically equal in IQ. Minor differences have been found among various groups; for example, the average score of Jews is somewhat higher than the overall norm. But within the middle class, such differences tend to be small. As the social class scale is descended from middle class to lower lower class, IQ scores decrease in step with attitudes, type of verbal interaction in the home, educational aspirations, and other factors that influence academic intelligence.

At various times in history, different ethnic and racial groups have been regarded as mentally inferior. Henry Goddard tested immigrants at Ellis Island some 50 years ago and reported that 80 percent were feebleminded; British Protestants have regarded Irish Catholics as innately shiftless and dumb. But in each case, changes in social conditions occurring over time have proved the supposition of a genetically inferior group to be incorrect.

Currently in America there is a disproportionately high percentage of blacks in the lower socioeconomic classes. And as a consequence, on the average, blacks score lower on IQ tests. The historical conditions—of racial prejudice and economic inequality—that have produced this situation are obvious. Remediation of the injustice has begun on two fronts. There is a move to eliminate discrimination in jobs and in economic opportunity, and this is being followed by changes in individual aspirations, material resources for education, and home conditions. There has also been an introduction of special academic programs to accelerate de facto integration by preparing the current generation of black students for technical and professional employment.

In his 1969 *Harvard Educational Review* paper, Arthur Jensen argued strongly that blacks are genetically inferior to whites in intelligence. Furthermore, Jensen's paper is said to have been used to justify the reduction of funds for government programs aimed at eliminating racial inequality. Shortly after the paper appeared, *Life* quoted then White House adviser Daniel Moynihan as saying that "the winds of Jensen were gusting through the capital with gale force." Such political ramifications make it important to emphasize that the hypothesis of genetically based racial differences in intelligence is far from proved. There are no direct biological data on the issue; the only support comes from studies comparing average IQ scores of various racial groups. Such studies do not in themselves reveal the source of group differences; in fact, a strong case can be made that racial and social class disparities in IQ arise from differential cognitive experience and orientation. Interestingly, one year prior to his *Harvard Educational Review* paper, Jensen himself marshalled an impressive body of evidence for the differential learning view in an article included in the book *Social Class, Race, and Psychological Development.* The following is an excerpt from Jensen's earlier article:

> One of the most thorough investigations of the relationship between reading readiness in first-grade children and patterns of parent-child interaction has been carried out by Esther Mil-

ner (1951). Milner specifically chose first-graders for her study, since home influences on verbal behavior are more manifestly prepotent at this educational stage than are school influences. All of the children in her study were Negro, ranging on an index of social status from lower-lower to lower-upper class. A composite score from a number of reading-readiness tests showed a correlation (Pearson *r*) of 0.86 with the social-class index. That is, dividing the children into high and low groups on the basis of reading readiness resulted in about the same two groups as when they were divided on the basis of social class. Through interviews with the children and their mothers a number of environmental differences between low and high scorers in reading readiness were discovered. Many of the differences seem to be directly related to verbal attainment. For example, it was found that the high-scoring children were surrounded by a richer verbal environment at home than the low-scoring children. More books were available to the high scorers, who also were read to by adults more than the low-scoring children. There also seemed to be more evidence of opportunities for emotionally positive interaction with the parents among the high scorers, and this often took place in a context favoring language development. For instance, mothers of low scorers indicated more frequently that as a rule they do not eat breakfast with their children or do not talk with the children during breakfast. The same was true for supper.

That much of the difference in reading readiness that Milner found between lower- and middle-class children was due to the kinds of environmental factors she describes has been shown experimentally by introducing certain middle-class practices into lower-class homes and later comparing these children with those from other lower-class homes in a matched control group. Irwin (reported in McCandless, 1961, p. 260), for example, had lower-class mothers read aloud to their children for at least ten minutes a day from the age of one, a practice that is common in the middle class but rare in the lower class. A control group of similar mothers was given no such instructions. Measures of language development showed significant differences between the experimental and control groups in all phases of speech by twenty months of age.

> Can a child's language level be changed by the age of entering nursery school or kindergarten? A study by Dawe (1942) suggests that it can be. Orphanage children ranging in age from 3 years 7 months to 6 years 10 months were given special speech and language training only on weekends for a total of ninety-two hours over a period of about 7½ months. Compared with a well-matched control group, the experimental group showed a gain of 14 IQ points (their mean initial IQ was about 80). The language training did not consist of mere test coaching; the transfer of training was quite general and showed up in a variety of assessment procedures.

In the 60-page paper from which this quotation is taken, Jensen emphasized three points: first, the social classes differ in the types of verbal stimulation and interaction that occur in the home; second, because of this, children from different social classes are markedly dissimilar in learned patterns of verbal organization; and third, these contrasting patterns of verbal organization could very likely form the basis of social class differences in IQ.

Jane Mercer and Wayne Brown recently completed a study that also examined some of the factors that give rise to racial differences in IQ test scores. As part of an elementary school desegregation program in Riverside, California, IQ tests were administered to Anglo children in the "receiving" schools, and to Mexican-American and black children in both segregated and integrated schools.

The Mexican-American children's average IQ on the Wechsler Intelligence Scale for Children (WISC) was 90.4. The black children had an average IQ of 90.5, and the Anglo children had an average IQ of about 107.

Mercer and Brown developed a five-item sociocultural modality index that measured the similarity of black and Mexican-American families to the modal middle-class Anglo family of the community. Children were statistically arranged according to this index. For example, a black child from a family that was similar to the modal Anglo community on four characteristics was assigned an index score of 4. Sociocultural index scores were then compared with IQ scores.

Among Mexican-American children, those having zero or 1 modal characteristic in their backgrounds had an average IQ of 84.5. Those with 2 modal characteristics had an average IQ of 88.1; those with 3 modal characteristics had an average IQ of 89; those with 4 modal characteristics had an average IQ of 95.5; and those with all 5 modal characteristics in their backgrounds had an average IQ of 104.4.

With black children the situation was nearly identical. Those whose family backgrounds were least like that of the modal Anglo family—reflected by an index score of 0 or 1—had an average IQ of 82.7. Those with an index score of 5 (family backgrounds comparable to that of the Anglo community) had an average IQ of 99.5, which is the national norm for the WISC. The fact that the average black score was a little below the scores of the Anglo and Mexican-American comparison groups will be discussed in more detail shortly.

On the whole, these data mean that statements such as "blacks have lower IQs than whites" or "Mexican-Americans have lower IQs than Anglos" are incorrect. Children from middle-class Mexican-American and black families have IQs that are basically equal to those of middle-class Anglo children. At present, the only well-documented statement is that IQ is related to socioeconomic position (and all the background experiences and learned values that entails).

The conditions characteristic of poverty homes described in Chapter III (restricted verbal interaction, physical disorganization) were just that—conditions of poverty homes. These were not Mexican-American homes, black homes, or German immigrant homes; they were low-socioeconomic-class homes. Middle- and upper-class black and Mexican-American homes are basically as middle and upper class as those of any other ethnic group. A study by Richard Bloom, Martin Whiteman, and Martin Deutsch, for example, has shown that while there are some important differences between socioeconomically matched blacks and whites in family activities, attitudes, and aspirations related to intellectual growth, in general "the relationship between social class and environmental conditions is similar in both [groups]." *

Mercer and Brown made a number of additional statistical analyses of the data obtained in the Riverside study, and all led to the same conclusion: The IQ differences between Anglo and minority group children were primarily attributable to sociocultural rather than biological factors. Furthermore, one of the simplest but most convincing arguments supporting this interpretation is the almost identical statistics obtained with blacks and Mexican-Americans. Since these two groups migrated to Riverside from different areas, it seems most unlikely that they had identical gene pools for intelligence. The more probable explanation is that similar sociocultural constraints acting on these minority group children in Riverside had parallel effects in depressing academic readiness or IQ.

In the light of Mercer and Brown's study—along with research evidence such as that cited by Jensen in the article quoted earlier—what support is there for the position that true biological differences in IQ exist among the races? Jensen's various published statements on racial differences (1969; 1973) show that the crux of his argument rests on two types of statistical comparisons. The first type of evidence comes from the comparison of the IQ scores of blacks with the IQ scores of whites, American Indians, Mexican-Americans, Orientals, and other groups who have been equated or matched on socioeconomic indices. Some studies have found that even after socioeconomic matching, blacks' scores remain a little below those of other groups. This tendency was noted in Mercer and Brown's study. The second type of evidence is that blacks tend to score slightly higher on verbal IQ tests than

*Quoted from a summary by Bloom, Davis, and Hess (1965).

on nonverbal tests, whereas other language-disadvantaged groups (for example, Mexican-American and Oriental children) show the opposite pattern. Jensen has used this to argue that the hypothesis of deficient language experience cannot explain the low IQ scores obtained by blacks.

In answering Jensen's first point, the prominent geneticist, Theodosius Dobzhansky, has argued that statistical matching of blacks with other groups on socioeconomic indices cannot be regarded as *total environment* matching and, therefore, that remaining IQ differences are not necessarily attributable to genetic makeup. He has quoted Walter Bodmer and Luigi Cavalli-Sforza on this point:

> It is difficult to see . . . how the status of blacks and whites can be compared. The very existence of a racial stratification correlated with relative socioeconomic deprivation makes this comparison suspect. Black schools are well known to be generally less adequate than white schools, so that equal numbers of years of schooling certainly do not mean equal educational attainments. Wide variation in the level of occupation must exist within each occupational class. Thus one would certainly expect, even for equivalent occupational classes, that the black level is on the average lower than the white. No amount of money can buy a black person's way into a privileged upper-class white community, or buy off more than 200 years of accumulated racial prejudice on the part of the whites. . . . It is impossible to accept the idea that matching for status provides an adequate, or even substantial, control over most important environmental differences between blacks and whites.

Among the "most important environmental differences between blacks and whites" mentioned by Bodmer and Cavalli-Sforza, one stands out with singular clarity: "No amount of money can buy a black person's way into a privileged upper-class white community." There is an extensive literature on what it means to be an American black. John McCarthy and William Yancey have shown that the exact effects on broad variables like self-esteem and self-hatred are complicated by various considerations—especially the reference group used for self-evaluation. Despite such complications, most researchers have agreed that in the broader culture, black skin is a strongly negative social factor. Some writers speak of a caste system in America—in contrast to socioeconomic class—that no black man can at present escape. A middle-income black, for example, is in many situations less accepted than a low-income American Indian or Eskimo. This extends beyond purely social relations. Consider the black man as a small businessman in a white community; or consider him as a door-to-door salesman, a real-estate salesman, or a manager in a primarily white company. In most cases he would meet with more obstacles than would an Oriental or a Mexican-American—greater feelings of doubt, resentment, suspicion, and uneasiness. In the American caste system the black man is at the very bottom, and far below other minorities. The effects of such limited horizons on the development of intelligence are inestimable.

Being black in America involves not only restrictive prejudices, but also a stereotype of mental incompetence. Thomas Pettigrew has explored some implications of this situation:

> Racist claims of Caucasian superiority contribute to the Negro's lack of intellectual self-confidence. This insecurity is especially provoked by any direct comparison with white performance. One investigation administered a task to Southern Negro college students with two different sets of instructions (Katz, Epps, and Axelson). One set told how other students at their college did on the task, while the second told how whites throughout the nation did. Those subjects who anticipated white comparison performed significantly more poorly on the task and indicated stronger concern and anxiety about their performance.
>
> The role of "Negro" is [also] a critical factor. Put simply, the Negro is not expected to be bright.

Robert Rosenthal conducted a series of studies showing that a teacher's expectations about the children in her class have a powerful effect on their individual mental growth. In one large and well-controlled experiment, teachers were given the names of certain children and told that on the basis of test scores these children were expected to make significant mental gains during the year. In actuality, children were selected for this experimental designation on a random basis. Apparently, however, the teachers provided extra attention, opportunity for response, and appropriate feedback to the anticipated bloomers. In comparison with the controls, the experimental children gained an average of 7 points on a nonverbal IQ test and 2 points on a verbal IQ test, for an overall gain of 4 IQ points. The 4-point increase was modest, but statistically significant and theoretically important.

Rosenthal drew on the results of an experiment by Eleanor Leacock in pointing out the implications this "Pygmalion effect" might have for the education of lower-income and black children:

> Eleanor Leacock studied four schools in four neighborhoods, two poor and two middle-income. Within each income level one school was essentially all black and the other essentially white. Leacock interviewed the fifth-grade teachers about their feelings for the children, and scored their comments for positive, neutral, or negative feelings and attitudes. . . .
>
> Leacock found that the teachers were much less favorable to the lower-class children than they were to the middle-class children; 40 percent of their comments about the poorer children were negative, compared to 20 percent of their comments about the middle-class children. And the teachers were even more likely to talk negatively about black children than white children, 43 percent to 17 percent.
>
> Leacock then went on to relate the children's IQ scores to the teachers' feelings toward them. IQ scores of the middle-income children, both black and white, were clearly related to the positive attitudes of their teachers. This relationship did not

hold for the low-income children; in fact, it was reversed. That is, lower-income children who had higher IQs tended to have teachers who viewed them negatively and this was especially true for lower-income children who were black. The children who surpassed their teachers' expectations got resentment and complaints for their pains.

Thus children who are both black and lower-income have a double handicap. And this result cannot be attributed to white teachers' bias; both of the teachers of the black children were themselves black. The prejudice of stunted expectations knows no race barrier.

Because it is impossible to evaluate fully the influences of racial stereotypes and prejudices on mental growth, a number of professional organizations, such as the American Psychological Association and the American Anthropological Association, have warned against drawing premature conclusions about racial differences in IQ. For example, the Society for the Psychological Study of Social Issues (a division of the APA) issued a statement calling Jensen's views on heredity and intelligence "unwarranted by the present state of scientific knowledge." It also noted that "a more accurate understanding of the contribution of heredity to intelligence will be possible only when social conditions for all races are equal, and when this situation has existed for several generations."

Consider now the second piece of evidence cited by Jensen to prove the genetic inferiority of blacks. Jensen noted that blacks tend to score slightly higher on verbal tests than on nonverbal tests of intelligence. By contrast, other verbally disadvantaged groups (Orientals, Mexican-Americans) show the opposite pattern. From this Jensen has argued that the low IQs of blacks are due not to a "verbally deficient environment" but rather to congenital incapacity. To examine this argument, we must first review a little psychometric theory.

Beginning with the early work of Spearman, psychometrists have shown that each type of IQ test item depends not only on intelligence, but also on certain more specific types of learning. For example, one of the Series Completion items (see Appendix 1) requires knowledge of fractions as well as reasoning ability; the Figural Reasoning item assumes that the examinee can visualize the geometrical pattern of rotation in organizing the relation—yet the ability to *visualize rotation* is to a large degree distinct from overall intelligence (French, 1951); and the Verbal Classification item depends on word knowledge along with analytical thinking. A simplified example will illustrate the differential growth of various abilities.

Consider an Oriental child brought up in a home where Chinese is spoken almost exclusively. Furthermore, assume that his parents are concerned and ambitious about present and future economic security, have a high regard for their child's education, and are themselves oriented toward careful thorough thinking (in contrast to one-shot thinking) in meeting economic and other day-to-day problems. Both parents live in the home, and other adults (uncles, aunts, grandparents) frequently play and talk with the child. In such a home, we should expect many of the adult-child verbal interactions to communicate information, ask and answer questions, explain causes of events, point to perceptual discriminations, classify objects by function or other significant characteristics —in general, form the basis of academic readiness when the child enters school. Of course, because most of the verbal exchange in the home is in Chinese, this child will be at a disadvantage in the English-speaking classroom. But in the long run, this type of disadvantage is usually overcome. Academic reasoning ability has been given a strong start, and topics in mathematics and science will tend to be learned without undue difficulty. However, vocabulary growth may lag behind that of children from native American middle-class homes. As reported, for instance, in Jensen's (1973) research, many such bilingual children score a little higher on nonverbal tests of intelligence than on verbal tests.

This example illustrates the distinction between two types

of verbally deficient early environments. The deficiency in the Chinese home just described is specific to English. There is no paucity of verbalized ideas. By contrast, the verbal deficiency of low IQ homes discussed by Bereiter and Engelmann (Chapter III) relates to how language is used in nurturing thinking patterns. Jensen failed to distinguish between these two different types of language deficiencies when he equated the verbal disadvantages of black and Oriental children and then concluded that black children must be genetically inferior since they score lower on nonverbal than verbal tests while Orientals exhibit the opposite pattern.

This discussion can be carried further. Vocabulary tests have been the most highly criticized measures of IQ. Educators have pointed out that some students (often those who are loquacious or "verbal types") memorize words and their meanings, and score inordinately well on verbal intelligence tests that depend heavily on vocabulary knowledge. This is a legitimate criticism. Vocabulary knowledge generally accumulates in the course of comprehending and reasoning with verbal material. However, vocabulary tests do not directly measure comprehension and reasoning ability in the way that verbal analogy, figural reasoning, and reading comprehension tests do. Thus a person of only modest reasoning ability can —if so oriented—memorize an extensive body of words and score well on conventional vocabulary tests. Such a person, irrespective of his race, would tend to score higher on verbal IQ tests than on nonverbal tests, since vocabulary knowledge usually helps to improve scores on many types of verbal intelligence scales. But this pattern of verbal score higher than nonverbal score in no way proves that the individual lacks innate mental endowment. It merely reflects the fact that one type of learning (verbal knowledge) is more highly developed than other types of learning (reasoning skill and basic geometrical-mathematical concepts involved in nonverbal tests).

At present it is difficult to pinpoint why, on the average, blacks tend to score slightly higher on verbal than on nonverbal IQ tests. Speculation suggests several reasons. Traditionally in America the better jobs open to blacks have not been in technical fields but in services and entertainment. In these occupations, appearances and social interaction are salient, and language facility is a most useful attribute. Not unrelated to this and to the general role of blacks in America, it appears that among blacks verbal fluency (a type of smooth, quick articulateness) is often valued and reinforced—much more so than, for example, arithmetic ability or technical reasoning. Under these conditions, the language patterns a black child develops as he moves out into the community could quite reasonably produce higher scores on verbal than nonverbal tests. But this is admittedly mere speculation.

More important, research has shown that black children's nonverbal reasoning ability can be improved through training. Thomas Pettigrew has reviewed some background research in the area and summarized two training experiments. (The *spatial visualization* and *spatial perception* abilities referred to are specialized facets of overall intelligence.)

> Woods and Toal matched two groups of Negro and white adolescents on IQ and noted sub-test differences. While superior to the whites on some tests, the Negroes were noticeably deficient on tasks such as detection of errors and drawing pictorial completions which required spatial visualization. And other similar studies reach the same conclusion (Bean; Clark; Franklin . . .). One demonstrated that this difficulty with perceptual and spatial relations was considerably more marked in a Southern-reared Negro sample than in an IQ-matched Northern-reared sample (Machover). This breakdown of spatial performance among otherwise intelligent Negro children, especially in the more restrictive South, offers a suggestive parallel with the comparable spatial breakdown noted in the sensory-deprivation research. In any event, two additional studies provide evidence that this disability is correctable (Boger; Eagleson). Both studies gave groups of Negro and white children special training in spatial perception and found that the Negro

subjects benefited more from the practice. IQ test scores were markedly higher for the Negro subjects five months after the training (Boger).

An experiment that Barry Guinagh conducted subsequent to Jensen's *Harvard Educational Review* paper also bears strongly on this point. Guinagh's experiment was addressed to the following statement made by Jensen in his paper: "I have found no studies that demonstrated gains [from training] in relatively noncultural or nonverbal tests like Cattell's Cultural Fair Tests and Raven's Progressive Matrices." In order to obtain data on this question, Guinagh selected groups of black and white low-socioeconomic-status third-graders from a school in Gainesville, Florida, and trained them on the concepts involved in Raven's Progressive Matrices. The first two sessions were on a one-to-one basis with the trainer, and in later sessions two children worked with a trainer. (The training used a task-analysis model as discussed by Robert Gagné.) Guinagh found that black children as well as white children made statistically significant gains on this nonverbal test of intelligence; moreover, the gains persisted on a retention test administered 1 month after the completion of training.

Guinagh's study also included an experimental condition that evaluated a somewhat technical aspect of Jensen's genetic-factors theory of IQ—and the results basically proved Jensen's theory wrong. The interested reader may refer to the original report for more details.

It seems clear that at present there is no conclusive answer to the question of whether the IQ test differences that currently exist among the races are to any degree genetic. However, as noted in Chapter VI, the question of whether genetic factors can produce IQ variations—either within a race or among races—is of only secondary interest to educators. The primary question is: What can be accomplished through education? If pedagogical methods can be found that allow all persons to assume a productive role in our literate-technical culture, then genetic differences—and any pieces of evidence that researchers such as Jensen, Herrnstein, and Shockley can offer to prove the existence of genetic differences—become largely irrelevant.

Jensen focuses on this primary question when he contends that programs of compensatory education are doomed to failure because they cannot counteract the overwhelming influence of genetic makeup on intelligence. However, the evidence appears not to bear him out. The Milwaukee Project supplies a strong counterargument to Jensen's contention, and further argument comes from the various other training experiments reviewed in Chapter III. Many children will need to be taught by the school how to comprehend, analyze, and integrate academic and technical materials. Appropriate learning-to-learn instructional methods are being developed and tested in a number of experimental programs. When perfected for incorporation into the entire educational system, these methods may give all children an equal chance for academic and professional success, irrespective of social class and home background. Much new research has accumulated, and many earlier findings are now better understood than they were in 1969 when Jensen wrote that "compensatory education has been tried and it apparently has failed." Contrary to this earlier conclusion, it now appears that the possibilities for training basic thinking capacities have only begun to be explored.

APPENDIX 1.

SAMPLE IQ TEST

QUESTIONS

One of the earliest findings of research in the area of mental testing was that a wide variety of questions can be suitably employed to scale intelligence. A person who performs well on any one task tends to perform well on the others.* As a consequence, most IQ tests include a few problems of several different types in order to obtain an overall estimate of mental ability.

Research has not only defined the many different tasks that do tap intelligence, it has also sorted out the types of human performances that are unrelated to it. Visual acuity and other sensory measures are unrelated. Reaction time and various pure speed measures show no connection. Even certain types of learning and memory abilities have been found to be distinct and separate from intelligence. Psychologists now agree that intelligence should not be regarded as overall neural efficiency or adaptiveness. Rather, it is confined to a specific (although not yet clearly defined) set of mental operations.

SAMPLE TEST ITEMS

I. Vocabulary (vocabulary scales appear on almost all intelligence tests. Several different formats are used.)

*The common ability underlying different items is represented as *g* by Spearman, as a higher-order factor by Lewis Thurstone, and as general intelligence by modern hierarchical theories of intellect. Lee Cronbach (1970) discusses the prominence of this capacity in Joy Guilford's model.

1. What is a *platitude?*

2. Select the word that has the closest meaning to the first word.
   histrionic A. antiquated B. legendary C. theatrical D. surgical

3. Select the word that means the opposite of the first word.
   demise A. hasty B. birth C. accept D. embrace

II. Verbal Classification

1. Select the word that is different from the other three words.
   A. peregrination B. pilgrimage C. outlandish D. promenade

III. Figure Classification

1. Select the figure which is different from the other four.

IV. Following Directions

1. If the circle below is taller than the square and the cross is shorter than the square put a *K* in the circle. However, if this is not the case, put a *C* in the second tallest figure.

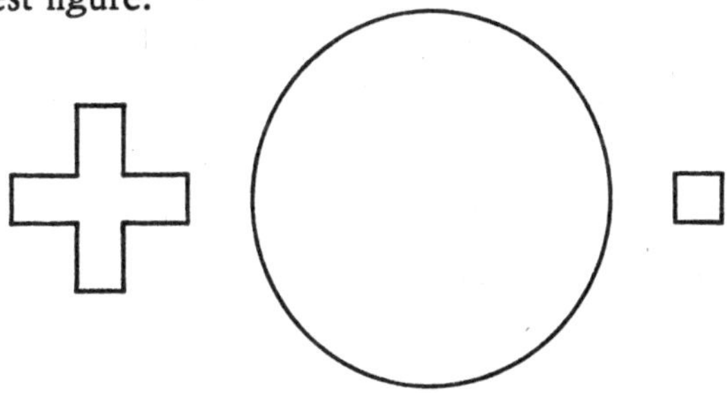

V. Sentence Completion

1. Select the pair of words that best fits the meaning of the sentence.

   Rational men must agree in the existence of a life after death. For without this there can be no justice—no reward for the______, who, through capricious fate, have had a hard lot in this world, nor condemnation for those ______ persons who have profited from their wrong acts.
   A. men-innocent B. people-lazy C. poor-many D. good-evil

VI. Verbal Analogies

1. *Hospital* is to *Sickness* as ______ is to ______.
   A. Patient-Disease B. Jail-Prisoner C. Doctor-Patient D. School-Ignorance E. Nurse-Illness

VII. Reading Passage Interpretation

A selection must be read and then a series of questions must be answered. Several examples are presented in Chapter IV.

VIII. Series Completion

1. Select the letter that should appear next in the series.
   C B F E I H L K __

2. Select the number that should appear next.
   1 ½ 4 2 7 3½ 10 5 ___

IX. Figural Reasoning

1. The top four figures in the illustration on the opposite page change in a systematic manner according to some rule. Your task is to discover the rule and choose from among the alternatives the figure which should occur next in the series.

X. Proverb and "Sayings" Interpretation

1. Show me the man you honor. I know by that symptom, better than any other, what you are yourself.—Carlyle

   Select the alternative that is most nearly equivalent in meaning.

   A. The works of great scholars should be read and studied.
   B. A man can be judged by his works.
   C. A man can be judged by those he emulates.
   D. Each human being has his own unique worth.

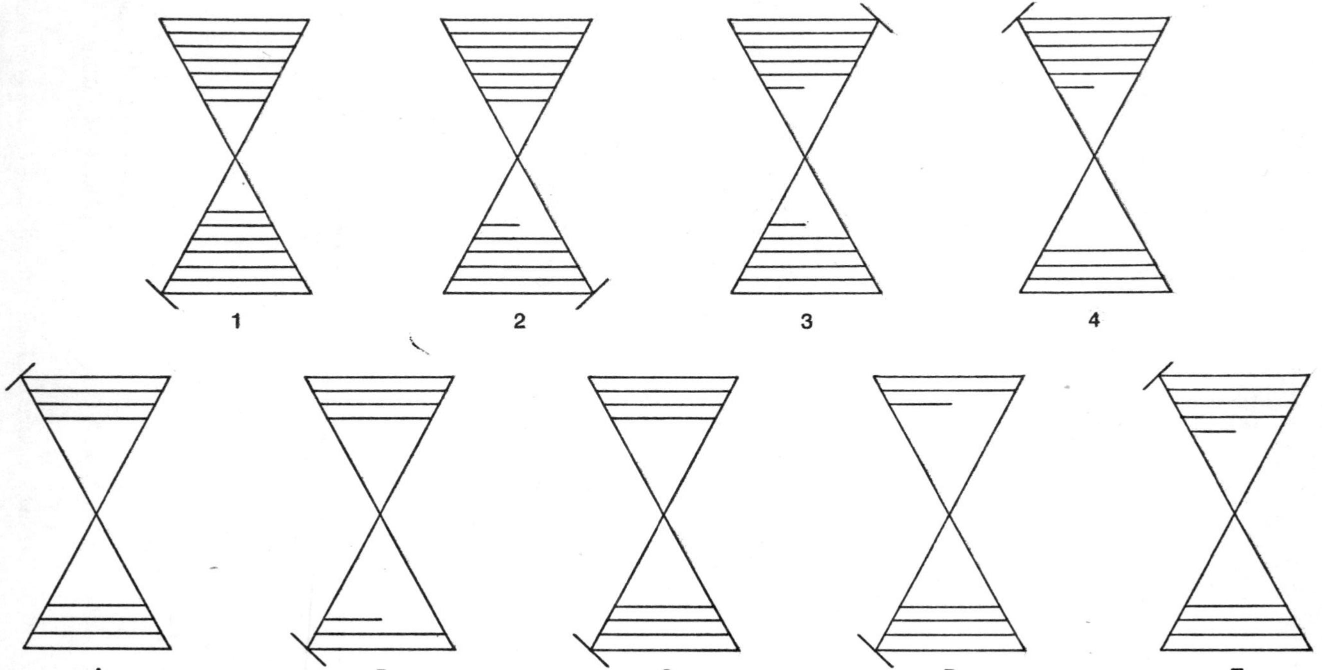

1 2 3 4

A B C D E

APPENDIX 2.

SAMPLE FROM REMEDIAL PROGRAM*

PRESENTATION	REASONS
TEACHER: [Presents picture of rifle] This is a ______.	She begins with no verbal explanation. Lengthy verbal preambles do not make learning easier or the material more meaningful to naïve children. They simply bore the child or entertain him in a passive nonproductive manner.
CHILD B: Gun. TEACHER: Good. It is a gun.	She would have favored the word *rifle* instead of *gun,* but since *gun* is correct and since the response was apparently the product of thinking, she uses *gun,* and she praises the child.
Let's all say it: This is a gun. This is a gun. Again. This is a gun.	The children seem uninterested. Learning will not proceed smoothly unless the

*From C. Bereiter and S. Engelmann. *Teaching Disadvantaged Children in the Preschool.*

teacher can secure the children's interest. Many motivating devices are possible, but the teacher prefers one that will favor the members of the class who are paying attention.

Let's say it one more time: This is an alligator.

CHILD D: It ain't neither. It a *gun.*

This device would not be recommended if the children had only a tenuous grasp of the concept. The teacher feels reasonably sure, however, that every child in the class knows what a gun is. The task, therefore, is a test of their attention, not their knowledge.

TEACHER: That's what I said. I said, "This is a bulldog."

All the children are interested now. They are aware of the sham battle of wits and they enjoy it, because they understand that they usually win.

CHILDREN (A, B, C, D, E): No, no. It ain't no bulldog. That a *gun.*

The children are laughing at the teacher. She pretends to be hurt.

TEACHER: Well, what did I say?

She has ordered the task so that the proof hinges on what was said. The children who attended to the presentation are the only ones who are in a position to apply the *coup de grâce.*

CHILDREN: You say that a bulldog.

The teacher apparently wilts, as the children laugh.

TEACHER: You're just too smart for me. You listen so big that I can't get away with a thing.

The moral: Knowledge is strength. If one thinks and remembers, he can even "outsmart" his teacher. (Moral 2: Even teachers are wrong sometimes.)

Okay, I'll start again. This is a gun. Is that right?

The children are attentive. Perhaps they are motivated out of a desire to catch the teacher in another mistake, but they are definitely motivated. So the teacher proceeds quickly. The common error beginning teachers make is to win children over and then feel obliged to "talk to them" at length. This technique is poor. The teacher has already spent over a minute winning the children. She does not want to lose them, so she moves very fast.

This is a weapon. This is a gun. This is a weapon.

CHILD D: No, it ain't no weapon.

The teacher realizes that she has made a strategic mistake. She has set the children up to catch her errors. Now when she tries to present a new name, the children suppose that she is still carrying on the game. She realizes that she should have introduced the object as a weapon and not as a gun in the first place. She introduced the gun statement first because she felt it would be better to acknowledge the object by the familiar name before introducing the class name.

TEACHER: [Presents pictures of knife, cannon, pistol] This is a weapon. This is a weapon. This is a weapon. These are weapons. Say it with me. This is a weapon. This is a weapon. This is a weapon. These are weapons. Let's hear that last one again. Make it buzz. These are weaponzzz.

She does not argue with Child D because she feels that little would be gained, and time would be lost. Instead, she resorts to a familiar presentation pattern that has been used in connection with labels. The use of this presentation, she feels, will demonstrate to the children that she is serious, that the game is over.

[Refers to knife] This weapon is a ______. Who knows?

CHILD E: A knife.

TEACHER: Yes, a knife. Let's say it. This weapon is a knife. Again. This weapon is a knife.

She beat the children to the punch. Before they could raise the objection that the first picture did not depict a weapon but a knife, the teacher presented a full acknowledgment in one statement. She demonstrated that it is, in fact, a weapon. At the same time, she allowed the children to show off their knowledge about the knife.

[Refers to cannon] This weapon is a ______. Who knows?

She phrases her questions so that the children can answer with a single word. Yet, her questions are phrased so that the single-word answer completes the statement "This weapon is a ______." She reinforces the statement even when she wishes to move fast.

CHILD C: Battle.

TEACHER: That's pretty good. You use this thing in a battle, but it's called a cannon. This weapon is a *cannon.* Say it, everybody. This weapon is a cannon.

She wants the child to know that she approves of the manner in which he is thinking, but that his answer is wrong. She rates his answer as a reasonable one, but follows with a clear correction.

Is this a *battle?* . . . No, this is *not* a battle. This weapon is a ______. Come on, tell me.

When a child makes a mistake of this kind, his mistake may be picked up by the other children, and will often be repeated by the child who made it. She therefore labors the identification of the cannon.

CHILDREN A AND D: Cannon.

The teacher notices that Child B is not forming state-

CHILD B: [Mumble.]

ments, but is trying to imitate the sounds made by Child A and Child D.

TEACHER: Boy, I'm really proud of A and D. Do you hear the way they are talking up? And are they ever thinking! I'm really proud of them.

The old adage about catching flies with honey applies to the classroom situation. The teacher could have put Child B on the carpet, which would have taken time and might have disgraced him for only a momentary lapse. If he persists, she will be forced into more direct means, but, for now, she selects the band-wagon motivating technique.

CHILD B: I'm thinkin' big.

CHILDREN A, C, D, E: Me too. Me too.

TEACHER: Okay, just keep it up. Here we go. [Refers to pictures] This is a weapon. This is a weapon. This is a weapon.

She reviews the new statements before introducing the new task.

CHILD A: I got a cannon at . . . [stops talking as teacher holds outstretched hand only a few inches in front of child's face].

The summary should be conducted at a fast pace, so that the pieces are brought together and the children see where they are. Interruptions at this point are costly. The child is discouraged when the teacher's hand is placed close to his face—a useful technique.

TEACHER: Here's the rule: [claps rhythmically] If you use it to hurt somebody, then it's a weapon. Again. If you use it to hurt somebody, then it's a weapon. Say it with me. If you use it to hurt somebody, then it's a weapon. One more time. If you use it to hurt somebody, then it's a weapon.

The teacher drills this rule until the children learn it. They have learned in connection with other rules that the teacher will expect them to use the rule in the next set of tasks. They also know that she thinks rules of this kind are important—so important that she will not relent until this one has been learned (assuming that the rule is not beyond them).

And if it's a weapon, what do you do with it? Do you tickle somebody with it?

CHILDREN: No.

TEACHER: Do you eat with it?

CHILDREN: No!

TEACHER: Well, if it's a weapon, do you use it to hurt somebody? Yes.

The teacher flips the rule so that the child will be prepared to handle task questions of the type "If it's a weapon, what do you do with it?" and "If you use something to hurt somebody, what do you call it?" She presents the *yes-no* questions first because they are the easiest. They represent a simple rephrasing of the question provided by the teacher. The teacher selects interesting examples for this task because interesting examples prompt the children to use the rule.

What do you use a gun for?

CHILD A: Shoot.

The teacher immediately presents applications of the rule.

TEACHER: That's good, A. And do you hurt somebody when you shoot him?

The response is correct, so the teacher acknowledges it as a correct response, even though she would rather have a child say "To hurt somebody."

CHILD C: Maybe kill im dead.

CHILD D: That hurt.

The children are quite interested, so the teacher allows them to volunteer information.

TEACHER: Yes, you use a gun to hurt somebody. And what's the rule? Come on, think. If you use it to hurt somebody, then it's a ______.

CHILD E: [Mumble.]

The teacher attempts to apply the rule. She structures the task so that the children must supply only a single word. They do not respond, which the teacher takes to mean that her presentation left something to be desired. The children were obviously motivated and interested. Presenting the task at this stage was probably premature. The children did not have sufficient practice in saying either the regular-order or the reverse-order rule. The teacher decides to adopt a more rigid procedure starting with the rule.

TEACHER: [Claps and smiles] Oh, it's a tough one. But I can say it. Listen. If you use it to hurt somebody, then it's a weapon. You use a gun to hurt somebody, so what do you know about it? It's a weapon. Because what's the rule? IF YOU USE IT TO HURT SOMEBODY, THEN IT'S A WEAPON. Let's hear it. IF YOU USE IT TO HURT SOMEBODY, ———.

CHILDREN: THEN IT'S A WEAPON.

The teacher puts on an act. She becomes entertaining, knowing that the children will need to work with the rule for a few minutes and knowing that such drill can become terribly drab if it is just "Say it after me" activity. She therefore yells and claps and talks as if the rule is *fun.* She encourages the children to shout with her.

TEACHER: I'm thinking of a rifle, and what do you use a rifle for? You use it to POW POW—hurt somebody. AND IF YOU USE IT TO HURT SOMEBODY, ———.

CHILDREN: THEN IT'S A WEAPON.

The teacher again presents the gun example, but this time in a much more structured manner. She is establishing a presentational format for processing a number of things. The children are familiar with this general approach.

TEACHER: So what do you know about a rifle? Is it a peanut?

CHILDREN: No, it's a weapon.

This step in reasoning, the teacher realizes, is quite difficult and probably beyond the ability of some of the children in the class. She therefore amends her *what* question (What do you know about a rifle?) with a more highly structured *yes-no* question. By presenting the *yes-no* question, the teacher can prompt the children and increase the possibility of correct answers.

TEACHER: I'm thinking of a cannon, and what's a cannon for? You use it to CA-POW—hurt somebody. And if you use it to hurt somebody, ______.

CHILDREN: Then it's a weapon.

The teacher moves fast. She is using statements that allow her to demonstrate the rule quickly, and she takes advantage of the chance to speed and enliven the presentation.

TEACHER: I'm thinking of a cow, and what is a cow for? Do you use a cow to hurt somebody? No. And if you don't use it to hurt somebody, then it is NOT a ______.

CHILDREN: Weapon.

The fast, rhythmical presentation tends to encourage repetition, both of tasks and of answers. The children tend to answer every statement with "Then it's a weapon." To prevent this presentation hypnotism, the teacher includes examples of things that are not weapons. These are as useful from a concept-building standpoint as from a presentation standpoint.

Appendix 3.

CAN POOR READERS READ FASTER?*

During the 1970–71 school year the Reading Foundation, a speed reading organization located in Chicago, obtained a $110,000 contract to operate a reading program for all seventh-grade students in the Compton Unified School District (near Los Angeles). The performance objective was as follows: Seventy-five percent of the students in the program would increase their reading speed five times over their beginning level with 10% better comprehension after 24 hours of instruction and 22 hours of outside reading.

The *Diagnostic Reading Tests* were used to evaluate student performance during the 3-month program. The 1,934 students' comprehension scores decreased slightly, from a mean of 5.2 (twentieth percentile) to a mean of 4.9 (twentieth percentile), while reading speed increased from a mean of 155 words per minute (twenty-fifth percentile) to a mean of 657 words per minute. Only 259 students (13%) increased their comprehension by 10% and their reading speed by five times over their beginning levels, falling far short of the 75% goal established in the contract.

A number of questionable evaluation procedures were used throughout the program. One of the more serious prob-

*From M. H. Dembo and D. A. Wilson, Research Notes. *Phi Delta Kappan,* May 1973.

lems occurred when the Reading Foundation requested a change in the administration of the reading-rate section of the posttest. This section requires a 3-minute reading interval to determine reading speed in words per minute (it was properly administered for the pretests). The foundation asked that the posttests be changed to 30 seconds, arguing that since the test was normed only to 333 words per minute it would be impossible to demonstrate a 500% increase in reading speed. For example, if a student read at 125 words per minute at the start of the program, it could not be shown that he might read at 625 words per minute at the completion of the program. Following this procedure, the words-per-minute rate at 30 seconds was multiplied by six (since there are six 30-second intervals in three minutes) to obtain each student's reading rate. The foundation assured the district that this change would not alter the test's validity or reliability.

To explore the reliability of this change in administration, a randomly selected group of 440 students (all of whom had completed the program in January) took additional tests in June. The students took the same reading test, using both a 3-minute and a 30-second interval to determine reading speed, on two consecutive days.

This group began in October reading at 150 words per minute (3-minute interval) and completed the program in January at 823 words per minute (30-second interval). In June their mean scores were 205 words per minute (3-minute interval) and 780 words per minute (30-second interval). The result of this testing questions the use of short reading periods (sprint speeds) to determine reading speed. It also suggests that the actual number of students reaching the performance objective is probably lower than the 13% reported.

The Reading Foundation used sprint speeds in two earlier "successful" programs. On February 27, 1970, the *New York Times* reported that the foundation, using an intensive 3-month program involving 90 fifth-graders in Brooklyn, increased reading speed 33 times, so that students were reading over 5,000 words per minute. Similar results were reported for another program in Chicago.

Apart from the evaluation procedures, there were some theoretical weaknesses in the program. Robert B. Ayres, president of the Reading Foundation, made a number of assertions not supported by empirical research: "Increasing the rate of reading, as we will see, results in increased and faster understanding of the material. . . . Slow readers have common personality flaws. . . . Slow and ineffective reading is directly traceable to early school training in reading aloud."

The program was developed originally for college students and adults, but is now used in inner-city schools with children having many reading problems. The foundation believes that word attack skill training alone is not sufficient for students above the sixth grade who are reading three or more grades below grade level, and that the "use of speed reading techniques to develop residual mental capacity to read is the most effective methodology to help the underachiever. . . ."

Due to the nature of the contract signed with the school district, the Reading Foundation received $99,010 out of the contracted amount of $110,000. It was another successful program—for them.

BIBLIOGRAPHY

ANASTASI, A. "Intelligence and Family Size." *Psychological Bulletin* 53 (1956): 187–209.

ANASTASI, A. *Psychological Testing.* 3rd ed. New York: Macmillan, 1968.

AUSUBEL, D.P. "How Reversible Are the Cognitive and Motivational Effects of Cultural Deprivation? Implications for Teaching the Culturally Deprived Child." In *Education of the Disadvantaged: A Book of Readings,* edited by A. H. Passow; M. Goldberg; and A. J. Tannenbaum. New York: Holt, Rinehart and Winston, 1967.

BARTLETT, F.C. *Thinking: An Experimental and Social Study.* New York: Basic Books, 1958.

BEREITER, C. "The Future of Individual Differences." *Harvard Educational Review* 39 (1969): 310–318.

BEREITER, C., and ENGELMANN, S. *Teaching Disadvantaged Children in the Preschool.* Englewood Cliffs: Prentice-Hall, 1966.

BINET, A. "Perceptions d'Enfants." *Revue de philologie* 30 (1890).

BINET, A. *Introduction à la psychologie expérimentale.* Paris: F. Alcan, 1894.

BINET, A. *Les Idées modernes sur les enfants.* Paris: Ernest Flamarion, 1909.

BLANK, M., and SOLOMON, F. "A Tutorial Language Program to Develop Abstract Thinking in Socially Disadvantaged Preschool Children." *Child Development* 39 (1968): 379–389.

BLOOM, B.S., and BRODER, L. *Problem-Solving Processes of College Students.* Chicago: University of Chicago Press, 1950.

BLOOM, B.S.; DAVIS, A.; and HESS, R. (eds.) *Compensatory Education for Cultural Deprivation: Based on Working Papers Contributed by Participants in the Research Conference On Education and Cultural Deprivation.* New York: Holt, Rinehart and Winston, 1965.

BLOOM, R.; WHITEMAN, M.; and DEUTSCH, M. "Race and Social Class as Separate Factors Related to Social Environment." *American Journal of Sociology* LXX (4) (1965): 471–476.

BLOOMFIELD, L., and BARNHART, C.L. *Let's Read, A Linguistic Approach.* Detroit: Wayne State University Press, 1961.

BODMER, W.F., and CAVALLI-SFORZA, L.L. "Intelligence and Race." *Scientific American* 223 (1970): 19–29.

BURT, C. "The Genetic Determination of Differences in Intelligence: A Study of Monozygotic Twins Reared Together and Apart." *British Journal of Psychology* 57 (1966): 137–153.

CARROLL, J. *Language and Thought.* Englewood Cliffs: Prentice-Hall, 1964.

CARVER, R. *Sense and Nonsense in Speed Reading.* Silver Spring: Revrac, 1971.

CATTELL, R.B. "The Fate of National Intelligence: Test of a Thirteen-Year Prediction." *Eugenics Review* 42 (1950): 136–148.

CHALL, J.S. *Learning to Read: The Great Debate.* New York: McGraw-Hill, 1967.

College Entrance Examination Board. *Effects of Coaching on Scholastic Aptitude Test Scores.* New York: CEEB, 1965.

College Entrance Examination Board. *College Board Student Bulletin.* New York: CEEB, 1972.

COOPER, R.M., and ZUBEK, J.P. "Effects of Enriched and Restricted Early Environments on the Learning Ability of Bright and Dull Rats." *Canadian Journal of Psychology* 12 (1958): 159–164.

CRONBACH, L.J. "The Two Disciplines of Scientific Psychology." *American Psychologist* 12 (1957): 671–684.

CRONBACH, L.J. *Essentials of Psychological Testing.* New York: Harper & Row, 1970.

DANIELS, N. "The Smart White Man's Burden." *Harper's* 247 (1973): 24–40.

DAWE, H.C. "A Study of the Effect of an Educational Program upon Language Development and Related Mental Functions in Young Children." *Journal of Experimental Education* 11 (1942): 200–209.

DEMBO, M.H., and WILSON, D.A. "Can Poor Readers Read Faster?" *Phi Delta Kappan* 54 (1973).

DENENBERG, V.H. (ed.) *The Development of Behavior.* Stamford: Sinauer, 1972.

DIXON, R. "Studies of the Eye Movements in Reading of University Professors and Graduate Students." *Studies in the Psychology of Reading. University of Michigan Monographs in Education* 4 (1951): 115–118.

DOBZHANSKY, T. "Differences Are Not Deficits." *Psychology Today* 7 (1973): 96–101.

EDFELDT, A.W. *Silent Speech and Silent Reading.* Chicago: University of Chicago Press, 1960.

Educational Testing Service. *Information Bulletin Graduate Record Examination Program.* Princeton: ETS, 1971.

FARR, R. "Measuring Reading Comprehension: An Historical Perspective." *Twentieth Yearbook of the National Reading Conference* (1970): 187–197.

FITTS, P.M., and POSNER, M.I. *Human Performance.* Belmont: Brooks/Cole, 1967.

FLEISHMAN, E.A., and HEMPEL, W.E., JR. "Changes in Factor Structure of a Complex Psychomotor Test as a Function of Practice." *Psychometrika* 19 (1954): 239–252.

FLEISHMAN, E.A., and HEMPEL, W.E., JR. "The Relation Between Abilities and Improvement with Practice in a Visual Discrimination Reaction Task." *Journal of Experimental Psychology* 49 (1955): 301–312.

FRENCH, J.W. "The Description of Aptitude and Achievement Tests in Terms of Rotated Factors." *Psychometric Monographs* no. 5 (1951).

FRY, E. *Reading Instruction for Classroom and Clinic.* New York: McGraw-Hill, 1972.

FULLER, J.L., and THOMPSON, W.R. *Behavior Genetics.* New York: Wiley, 1960.

GAGNÉ, R. "The Acquisition of Knowledge." *Psychological Review* 69 (1962): 465–568.

GODDARD, H.H. "The Binet Tests in Relation to Immigration." *Journal of Psychoasthenics* 18 (1913): 105–107.

GODDARD, H.H. "Mental Tests and the Immigrant." *Journal of Delinquency* 2 (1917): 243–277.

GOLDSTEIN, K. *Human Nature in the Light of Psychopathology.* Cambridge: Harvard University Press, 1940.

GRAF, R.B. "Speed Reading: Remember the Tortoise." *Psychology Today* 7 (1973): 112–113.

GRUBER, G.R. *Reading Interpretation in Social Studies, Natural Sciences and Literature.* New York: Simon and Schuster, 1971.

GUILFORD, J.P. *The Nature of Human Intelligence.* New York: McGraw-Hill, 1967.

GUINAGH, B.J. "An Experimental Study of Basic Learning Ability and Intelligence in Low-Socioeconomic-Status Children." In *Educating the Disadvantaged,* edited by R.C. Doll and M. Hawkins. New York: AMS Press, 1971.

HADAMARD, J. *An Essay on the Psychology of Invention in the Mathematical Field.* Princeton: Princeton University Press, 1945.

HARDYCK, C.D., and PETRINOVICH, L.F. "Treatment of Subvocal Speech During Reading." *Journal of Reading* 12 (1969): 361–368; 419–422.

HARLOW, H.F. "The Formation of Learning Sets." *Psychological Review* 56 (1949): 51–65.

HAYES, K.J. "Genes, Drives, and Intellect." *Psychological Reports* 10 (1962): 299–342.

HEBB, D.O. "Man's Frontal Lobes." *AMA Archives of Neurological Psychiatry* 54 (1945): 10–24.

HEBB, D.O. "The American Revolution." *American Psychologist* 15 (1960): 735–745.

HEBER, R.; GARBER, H.; HARRINGTON, S.; HOFFMAN, C.; and FALENDER, C. *Rehabilitation of Families at Risk for Mental Retardation.* Progress Report. Rehabilitation Research and Training Center in Mental Retardation, University of Wisconsin, Madison, 1972.

HERRNSTEIN, R.J. *I.Q. in the Meritocracy.* Boston: Little/Brown, 1973.

HILGARD, E.R. Preface to *Social Class, Race, and Psychological Development,* edited by M. Deutsch; I. Katz; and A.R. Jensen. New York: Holt, Rinehart and Winston, 1968.

HOLMS, J. "The Substrata-Factor Theory of Reading: Some Experimental Evidence." In *Issues and Innovations in the Teaching of Reading,* edited by J.L. Frost. Glenview: Scott/Foresman, 1967.

HUNT, J. MCV. *Intelligence and Experience.* New York: Ronald Press, 1961.

JENCKS, C.; SMITH, M.; ACLAND, H.; BANE, M.J.; COHEN, D.; GINTIS, H.; HEYNES, B.; and MICHELSON, S. *Inequality: A Reassessment of the Effect of Family and Schooling in America.* New York: Basic Books, 1972.

JENSEN, A.R. "Transfer between Paired-Associate and Serial Learning." *Journal of Verbal Learning and Verbal Behavior* 1 (1962): 269–280.

JENSEN, A.R. "Social Class and Verbal Learning." In *Social Class, Race, and Psychological Development,* edited by M. Deutsch; I. Katz; and A.R. Jensen. New York: Holt, Rinehart and Winston, 1968.

JENSEN, A.R. "How Much Can We Boost I.Q. and Scholastic Achievement?" *Harvard Educational Review* 39 (1969): 1–123. (Also, *Harvard Educational Review,* Reprint Series no. 2 [1969]: 1–123.)

JOHNSON, D.M. "Application of the Standard-Score I.Q. to Social Statistics." *Journal of Social Psychology* 27 (1948): 217–227.

JUEL-NIELSEN, N. "Individual and Environment: A Psychiatric-Psychological Investigation of Monozygous Twins Reared Apart." *Acta psychiatrica et neurologica Scandinavica* (Monograph Supplement, no. 183), 1965.

KAGAN, J. "The Deprived Child: Doomed to Be Retarded?" *Los Angeles Times* (Feb. 25, 1973, Part VI), p. 1.

KAGAN, J.; SONTAG, L.W.; BAKER, C.T.; and NELSON, V.L. "Personality and IQ Change." *Journal of Abnormal and Social Psychology* 56 (1958): 261–266.

KAMIN, L.J. "Heredity, Intelligence, Politics, and Psychology." Paper available from the author. Department of Psychology, Princeton University, 1973.

KARNES, M.B. "Evaluation and Implications of Research with Young Handicapped and Low-Income Children." In *Compensatory Education for Chil-*

dren, Ages 2 to 8, edited by J.C. Stanley. Baltimore: The Johns Hopkins University Press, 1973.

KARNES, M.B.; HODGINS, A.S.; STONEBURNER, R.L.; STUDLEY, W.M.; and TESKA, J.A. "Effects of a Highly Structured Program of Language Development on Intellectual Functioning and Psycholinguistic Development of Culturally Disadvantaged Three-Year-Olds." *Journal of Special Education* 2 (1968): 405–412.

KARNES, M.B.; STUDLEY, W.M.; WRIGHT, W.R.; and HODGINS, A.S. "An Approach for Working with Mothers of Disadvantaged Preschool Children." *Merrill-Palmer Quarterly* 14 (1968): 174–184.

KARNES, M.B.; TESKA, J.A.; and HODGINS, A.S. "The Successful Implementation of a Highly Specific Preschool Instructional Program by Paraprofessional Teachers." *Journal of Special Education* 4 (1970): 69–80.

KLAUS, R.A., and GRAY, S.W. "The Early Training Project for Disadvantaged Children: A Report after Five Years." *Monographs of the Society for Research in Child Development* 33, no. 4 (1968).

KOLERS, P. "Experiments in Reading." *Scientific American* 227 (1972): 84–91.

LEWONTIN, R.C. "Race and Intelligence." *Bulletin of Atomic Scientists.* March, 1970, pp. 2–8.

LOBAN, W. "Oral Language Proficiency Affects Reading and Writing." In *Issues and Innovations in the Teaching of Reading,* edited by J.L. Frost. Glenview: Scott/Foresman, 1967.

MARRON, J.E. *Special Test Preparation, Its Effect on College Board Scores and the Relationship of Effected Scores to Subsequent College Performance.* Office of the Director of Admissions and Registrar, U.S. Military Academy, West Point, N.Y., November 1, 1965.

MCCARTHY, J.D., and YANCEY, W.L. "Uncle Tom and Mr. Charlie: Metaphysical Pathos in the Study of Racism and Personal Disorganization." *Educating the Disadvantaged,* edited by R.C. Doll and M. Hawkins. New York: AMS Press, 1971.

MCGUIGAN, F.J.; KELLER, B; and STANTON, E. "Covert Language Responses During Silent Reading." *Journal of Educational Psychology* 55 (1964): 339–343.

MERCER, J.R., and BROWN, W.C. "Racial Differences in I.Q.: Fact or Artifact." In *The Fallacy of I.Q.,* edited by C. Senna. New York: The Third Press, 1973.

MILLER, N.E. "Studies of Fear as an Acquirable Drive. I. Fear as Motivation and Fear-Reduction as Reinforcement in the Learning of New Responses." *Journal of Experimental Psychology* 38 (1948): 89–101.

NEWELL, A., and SIMON, H.A. *Human Problem Solving.* Englewood Cliffs: Prentice-Hall, 1972.

NEWMAN, H.H.; FREEMAN, F.N.; and HOLZINGER, K.J. *Twins: A Study of Heredity and Environment.* Chicago: University of Chicago Press, 1937.

PAGE, E.B. "Miracle in Milwaukee: Raising the IQ." *Educational Researcher* 1 (10) (1972): 8–16.

PETTIGREW, T.F. *A Profile of the Negro American.* New York: D. Van Nostrand, 1969.

PIAGET, J. *The Psychology of Intelligence.* Translated by M. Piercy and D.E. Berlyne. London: Routledge & Kegan Paul, 1947.

POLLACK, R.H., and BRENNER, M.W. (eds.) *The Experimental Psychology of Alfred Binet: Selected Papers.* New York: Springer, 1969.

POULTON, E.C. "British Courses for Adults on Effective Reading." *British Journal of Educational Psychology* 31 (1961): 128–137.

ROSENTHAL, R. "The Pygmalion Effect Lives." *Psychology Today* 7 (1973): 56–63.

SARASON, S.B. *Psychological Problems in Mental Deficiency.* New York: Harper, 1959.

SCOTT, J.P., and CHARLES, M.S. "Some Problems of Heredity and Social Behavior." *Journal of Genetic Psychology* 48 (1953): 209–230.

SEARLE, L.V. "The Organization of Hereditary Maze-Brightness and Maze-Dullness." *Genetic Psychological Monographs* 39 (1949): 279–325.

SENNA, C. (ed.) *The Fallacy of I.Q.* New York: The Third Press, 1973.

SHIELDS, J. *Monozygotic Twins Brought Up Apart and Brought Up Together.* London: Oxford University Press, 1962.

SHOCK, N.W., and JONES, H.E. "The Relationship between Basal Physiological Functions and Intelligence in Adolescents." *Psychological Bulletin* 36 (1939): 642–643.

SIMON, H.A., and CHASE, W.G. "Skill in Chess." *American Scientist* 61 (1973): 394–403.

SMITH, S. "Language and Non-Verbal Test Performance of Racial Groups in Honolulu before and after a Fourteen-Year Interval." *Journal of Genetic Psychology* 26 (1942): 51–93.

SOKOLOV, A.N. *Inner Speech and Thought.* New York: Plenum Press, 1972.

SONTAG, L.W.; BAKER, C.T.; and NELSON, V.L. "Mental Growth and Personality Development." *Monographs of the Society for Research in Child Development* 23, no. 2 (whole no. 68) (1958).

SPEARMAN, C. *The Abilities of Man: Their Nature and Measurement.* New York: Macmillan, 1927.

STANLEY, J.C. (ed.), *Preschool Programs for the Disadvantaged.* Baltimore: The Johns Hopkins University Press, 1972.

STANLEY, J.C. (ed.), *Compensatory Education for Children, Ages 2 to 8.* Baltimore: The Johns Hopkins University Press, 1973.

"Stop Trying to Teach Reading—Just Let It Happen, Expert Says." *Los Angeles Times* (Feb. 25, 1973), p. 3.

STRICKLAND, R.G. "The Contribution of Linguistics in Reading, Spelling, Grammar." In *Issues and Innovations in the Teaching of Reading,* edited by J.L. Frost. Glenview: Scott/Foresman, 1967.

STRICKLAND, S. "Can Slum Children Learn?" In *The Fallacy of I.Q.*, edited by C. Senna. New York: The Third Press, 1973.

TERMAN, L.M. *The Measurement of Intelligence.* Boston: Houghton Mifflin, 1916.

THORNDIKE, E.L. "Reading as Reasoning: A Study of Mistakes in Paragraph Reading." *Journal of Educational Psychology* 8 (1917): 323–332.

THURSTONE, L.L. "Second-Order Factors." *Psychometrika* 9 (1944): 71–100.

TINKER, M.A. *Bases for Effective Reading.* Minneapolis: University of Minnesota Press, 1965.

TINKER, M.A., and MCCULLOUGH, C.M. *Teaching Elementary Reading.* 2nd ed. New York: Appleton-Century-Crofts, 1962.

TRYON, R.C. "Genetic Differences in Maze Learning in Rats." *Yearbook of the National Society for the Study of Education* 39 (I) (1940): 111–119.

TUDDENHAM, R.D. "Soldier Intelligence in World Wars I and II." *American Psychologist* 3 (1948): 149–159.

TURNER, D.R. *Law School Admission Test.* New York: Arco, 1972.

United Nations. *Proceedings of the World Population Conference, Rome, 1954.* New York: United Nations, Department of Social Affairs, 1955.

VARON, E.J. "Alfred Binet's Concept of Intelligence." *Psychological Review* 43 (1936): 32–58.

WARK, D.M. "Reading Comprehension as Implicit Verbal Behavior." *Seventeenth Yearbook of the National Reading Conference* (1968): 192–198.

WATSON, J.B. *Behaviorism.* New York: W.W. Norton, 1924.

WECHSLER, D. *The Measurement of Adult Intelligence.* 3rd ed. Baltimore: Williams & Wilkins, 1944.

WHIMBEY, A.E., and DENENBERG, V.H. "Programing Like Histories: Creating Individual Differences by the Experimental Control of Early Experiences." *Multivariate Behavioral Research* 1 (1966): 279–286.

"Why Johnny Can't Read." *Newsweek* (Dec. 11, 1972), p. 122.

WOODROW, H. "Interrelations of Measures of Learning." *Journal of Psychology* 10 (1940): 49–73.

YARBROUGH, M.E., and MCCURDY, H.G. "A Further Note on Basal Metabolism and Academic Performance." *Journal of Educational Psychology* 49 (1958): 20–22.

YERKES, R.M. (ed.) "Psychological Examining in the U.S. Army." *Memoirs of National Academy of Science* 15 (1921).

INDEX